Spiraling Upward

THE 5 CO-CREATIVE POWERS FOR POWERS FOR WOMEN ON THE RISE

Wendy Wallbridge

bibliomotion
books + media

First published by Bibliomotion, Inc.
39 Harvard Street
Brookline, MA 02445
Tel: 617-934-2427
www.bibliomotion.com

Printed in the United States of America

Library of Congress Cataloging-in-Publication Data

Wallbridge, Wendy.
    Spiraling upward : the 5 co-creative powers for women on the rise / Wendy Wallbridge.
        pages cm
    Summary: "Using her "Spiral Up" method, Wallbridge teaches women to cultivate the five co-creative powers of energy, thoughts, feelings, speech, and action. This method encourages each reader to create a fulfilling life aligned with her own gifts and callings"— Provided by publisher.
    ISBN 978-1-62956-067-0 (hardback) — ISBN 978-1-62956-068-7 (ebook) — ISBN 978-1-62956-069-4 (enhanced ebook)
    1. Women—Vocational guidance.   2. Career development.   3. Success.   4. Self-realization in women.   I. Title.
    HF5382.6.W35 2015
    650.1082—dc23
                        2015000505

For my mom, who taught me how to love

CONTENTS

THE FIRST TURNING
Initiation

THE SECOND TURNING
Aspiration

THE THIRD TURNING
Inspiration

CHAPTER 1

Why Spiral Up?

In order to become free...it is important to simultaneously let go and move forward.
—Angeles Arrien

Half a century ago, women began to master the masculine path to success. And it's good that we did. This effort has afforded women in the West a level of financial freedom, privilege, and influence that would have been unimaginable just a few decades ago. American women comprise over half of management, professional and related positions in our workplaces and control trillions of dollars in the nation's economy, a figure which will continue to grow.

Never before in history have women been so degreed or so represented as decision makers in the economic and political sectors of the world. This is an exciting, even breathtaking, time to be a woman. So why are so many of us still sitting on the sidelines? Why are we rising only so far before we decide it's just not worth it? What's stopping us from unleashing our gifts in the world?

Twenty-five years of coaching professional women has taught me that while women have become masters at getting "A's"—approval, accolades, applause, achievements, and acquisitions—we become disillusioned because no amount of external validation can give us the experience of *wholehearted* success. This proclivity toward the linear (or as I call it, horizontal) path of accomplishment, at all costs, is devoid of the central ingredient needed for us to feel fulfilled. Most women are not drawn to power for power's sake. What matters more to us than ambition is meaning.

We can spend years, our whole career even, trying to convince others of our value or seeking fulfillment doing what someone else deems important.

But one day that external motivation runs out. What used to excite us about our work no longer does, and we wonder what's wrong with us. No matter the kudos we receive, until we are doing our soul's work, we will never be fulfilled.

This is the critical crossroads. No longer able to tolerate a life that's inauthentic, we arrive at a moment of truth. We can ignore the signs and push on. Or we can take the time to excavate our unique strengths, passions, and true nature in order to live from the core of who we are on behalf of all that we were meant to be.

If you have picked up this book, I believe that you are ready to rise to your full potential and live a richer, more meaningful life. The trouble is that our unique paths as women do not follow a straight line. Women are not meant to march on the masculine linear path to success. Our culture's emphasis on productivity is a demanding taskmaster. It prioritizes perfection over wholeness and efficiency over love. But deep down we know that material and external success without personal fulfillment is failure. We are meant to live spherically, wholly, and to expand outward rather than one dimensionally.

This journey of courageous reinvention is seldom validated by our society; in fact, it can be easily trampled on and even sabotaged. So while we want to rise—become more visible, speak truth to power, come out of the shadows to become the protagonist in our own story—we often let our fears about what others think of us dictate what we do. In order to diverge from the officially sanctioned path to success, we must first believe in ourselves and sponsor our heartfelt dreams. And, let's admit it, we've spent much of our life with our attention riveted on the surface of things, our exterior. To get where we want to go next, we'll need to mine the treasure chest within.

At this moment in history, when our voices are so desperately needed, a new approach—one that mirrors the evolution and expansiveness of life—is essential if we are to realize our greatest joy and contributions. *Spiraling Upward: The 5 Co-Creative Powers for Women on the Rise* offers a new road map for women to claim our wholeness and power in order to make an impact on our workplace, family, community—or wherever we feel called. *Spiraling Upward* teaches us how to put our masculine strengths in service to our feminine—that is, in service to what really matters to us—enabling us to consciously create a heightened and irresistible destiny.

But why specifically is it critical for *you* to rise? What is at stake for *you* personally? If you are like so many of the women I meet, you are ready to live beyond the constraints of your current reality and express yourself in a way that feels creative, authentic, and connected to the greater whole. You want to wake up to who you are within the world. You know the consequences of recycling old patterns and suppressing your wild soul's desires. And you know that you have gifts and talents that the world has never seen. If any of those reasons ring true, you have arrived at the right place.

Unlike rising to power in government or the corporate world (though those things may also be part of your path), rising to power in your *self* means coming into possession of your own gifts so that you can fulfill your potential and live your soul's purpose. It means doing the inner work that's needed to tap into the radiant and unlimited power you already hold. And when you do, nobody can take it away from you. And nothing can stop you.

It has been said that the teacher who is indeed wise does not ask that you enter the house of her wisdom, but rather leads you to your own. This book will guide you again and again to the wisest part of yourself and provide you with the tools and inspiration to become a powerfully conscious co-creator. You will learn what it really means to *lead* your life by becoming intentional in the five Co-Creative Powers of energy, thought, feelings, words, and actions— the fundamentals of self-creation.

In the chapters ahead, you'll engage in a process—tested and proven—that is itself a spiral: a cyclical journey of self-inquiry, self-discovery, and application. You will gain tools for replacing self-doubt with self-agency and for expressing your creativity and power. And as you progress on the journey, you will move from the limited definition of yourself based on your ego (roles, beliefs, negative judgments) to a more integrated, heart-centered, unabashedly self-expressed woman who feels a sense of belonging in the world.

At this pivotal moment, you are being invited to live your true destiny— to re-author your inherited scripts and wholeheartedly believe in yourself, to make your voice heard, to offer your gifts and talents fully. You are being invited to Spiral Up! toward a new definition of power and leadership.

But first, let me tell you my story.

Leaving the Horizontal Path

I was twenty-four years old when my life spiraled out of control.

Up to that moment, I had been barreling along on the fast track. I had started a successful company with two physicians, and I was living in a beautiful mansion overlooking the San Francisco Bay. One of the doctors began courting me and filled my house with flowers while trying to convince me to marry him.

I was just barely out of college and had already surpassed every goal I'd ever imagined. But success came at a cost. Like most of the people I knew, I was caught up in the party lifestyle of the '80s, and had started drinking and doing "recreational" drugs. I was running on fumes and ego—until the morning I woke up and could not move.

I lay there in my beautiful house, stricken and terrified. Every muscle of my body seared with pain as I tried to lift myself up. I called out for my roommate in a voice that barely sounded like mine. I only hoped that she could hear me.

Within hours I was sitting in the examining room of a noted rheumatologist. A round of tests confirmed my boyfriend's suspicion: I had lupus, a dangerous, unpredictable autoimmune blood disease that would eventually destroy my kidneys and require a transplant to save my life.

The physical pain was often severe—swollen joints, bone-wrenching fatigue, and inflammation of my organs—but the internal pain was greater still. The disease stripped away my ability to earn money, to prove myself, to stay in control so that I could make my life "perfect." I had built my identity around being an overachiever. In truth, I prided myself on how—in partnership with the doctors in my business—we had pioneered ways to bring the concepts of the human potential movement into health care and business. I had thought of myself as cool, cutting-edge. Now I felt worthless—and lost—as I faced questions I'd never entertained before in my full-speed-ahead, goal-directed life: Where do I go from here? Where do I turn? Who am I?

In the years after my diagnosis, while my friends climbed the corporate ladder or traveled to far-off places, I immersed myself in attempts to heal from this life-threatening illness. A student of the New Age, I believed that you "create" your life, but combining that philosophy with my Catholic upbringing proved lethal: it left me thinking, "If my life isn't the way I want it to be, then I have only myself to blame." Besides following my doctor's advice, I tried all kinds of alternative modalities to fix what *must* be wrong with me. I primal-screamed, tried rebirthing, bioenergetics, auditing, NLP, acupuncture, homeopathy, yoga, meditating, and journaling; I went into therapy, did twelve-step work, had monks *om* over me, and read rooms full of books, trying to discover my authentic self. While I grew and learned a lot, my internal "not enoughness" remained unchanged.

A turning point came when I realized the metaphor of my disease: an autoimmune disease in which my body misread its own tissue and attacked itself. Who had I become that I was a foreigner to myself?

As I began to delve into that question, I reflected on my early life. One summer night when I was sixteen years old, my mother totaled her car while drinking and almost died. In my disgust for my mom's alcoholic behavior, I rejected everything I associated with her, including my own feminine side. I tried to become the person I thought my dad needed—quiet and productive, someone to counterbalance the chaos. Throughout school and college I strove to get good grades and excel at any task in front of me. I operated under the imperative that I needed to "get it right." But that imperative was totally at odds with what my soul wanted: to have experiences, to make mistakes, to grow stronger from them, to be free.

Dealing with the relentless setbacks of my illness forced me to let go of my agenda. My honed ability to "make things happen" was useless when it came to finding peace in this situation. Something new was being invited forward in me. Lupus was a powerful force on the spiral path of my own evolution. In response to the brutality of my own self-derision, a deep compassion for others and myself was born.

Fourteen years after my diagnosis, the disease had progressed and my kidneys shut down. I required dialysis three times a week. At that point, the faith that I was developing in the way of the world—that there was a greater intelligence and that everything didn't fall on my shoulders—became even more critical. Placed on a donor list for a kidney transplant, I kept telling myself that a match would be found. One night, after a year and a half of waiting, the phone rang at two in the morning. The transplant nurse told me that a young man in Kentucky had just died. His kidney was the perfect match for me.

Within six months of my surgery, I wasn't only physically strong, I felt confident enough to take a leap of faith from my job and begin a coaching practice—and this, in 1992, before coaching had been established. Many of the high-achieving women who came to me reminded me of my old way of being, which I had learned from my dad.

I remember my father coming home exhausted every night. He worked from dawn till dusk building roads and highways. He knew everything about the straight path. "Wendy," he would say to me, "you can't always do what you want to do." I almost died trying to follow his path. I wanted so much to get his approval. But I needed to build my own road to success, one that inspired and nourished me. And so, the Spiral Up! process was born.

The Spiral: The Shape of Transformation

The most widespread and successful shape in nature, the spiral is present in everything from the swirl of galaxies to the structure of our own DNA helix. It gathers its force from the synergy of seeming opposites—the way two opposing air flows make a hurricane swirl—and from the very path it traces. Not simply forging ahead, the spiral turns back repeatedly in a natural cycle of contraction and expansion, ebb and flow; not just climbing up, it levels off only to come around again in a sweep that is higher and wider each time.

In a similar way, we keep encountering the same challenges and situations, and yet each time is a new opportunity to release old patterns and respond in a more conscious way. We are always drawing to us life experiences to awaken, evolve, and elevate us. When something interrupts our life—whether it's discontent or a full-blown crisis—we always have a choice: we can resist and begin the slow leak of our aliveness and spiral down, or we can transform to uplift.

We've all heard the term spiral down, but what does it mean in this context? There is a downward pull on us—just like rain or gravity—that starts in our minds. We've all experienced a moment, a day, or even longer where we lose our mojo, our confidence bottoms out, and everything appears as if through dark-colored glasses. Sometimes the feeling snowballs to encompass all the other reasons our life isn't working.

This tendency toward the negative isn't our fault. An undercurrent of worry and unease, and a sense we must guard against potential threats, got hardwired into our reptilian brain long ago to keep our ancestors alive. Our spirit, however, has a different agenda. It wants us to rise up and create lives of profound joy and positive influence. But unless we have an intimate experience of who we truly are, the ability to uplift can remain elusive. If we don't learn how to Spiral Up!, by default we will be dragged down by the free-floating fear, doubt, and worry that threaten to rob us of the contentment that lies at our core.

CHAPTER 2

Choosing the Spiral Up! Path

The greater the contrast, the greater the potential. Great energy only comes from a correspondingly great tension between opposites.

—C. G. Jung

The Spiral Up! path is the activation of two opposite forces—our generative masculine and our receptive feminine. Engaging and integrating these two forces creates a dynamic balance that takes our lives to the next level. The sacred feminine—the principle of connection—allows us to be touched by life's triumphs and difficulties and in the process reconnects us to the passion and intuition of our hearts. In response, our divine masculine enables us to take risks and act on behalf of our enlightened self.

Neither the masculine nor feminine is enough on its own: we can focus on a goal until we are bleary-eyed, but until we allow ourselves to receive it (to feel that we deserve it), it evades us; or we can feel worthy of our desire, but until we take steps to achieve it, we are left wistful and wanting. Through this marriage of opposites, we are introduced to a new way of living: when your dynamic, intentional energy husbands and supports, rather than stomps over, your intuitive, receptive feminine nature you naturally evolve and grow.

Becoming skilled in these two sets of strengths creates a dynamic balance that replaces effort with flow and activates an unstoppable power that inspires us to use our talents on behalf of the greater good. We no longer race along the linear path; we expand to live life wholly. In discovering the power of the spiral, my clients have achieved a level of success and fulfillment that they would previously have thought unimaginable.

A high-powered business leader who had achieved every imaginable symbol of success felt empty and exhausted. She admitted to showing up one way at work and another at home, and in neither place was she being her true self. As she evolved through the Spiral Up! process, the Co-Creative Power of **Energy** equipped her to confront the costs of being inauthentic and to unlock reserves of vitality and excitement by claiming and expressing her full-out, unbridled self.

Six months into Spiral Up!, a PhD-holding manager, who was consistently overlooked at work and didn't believe in the power of intention to manifest, began, through the Co-Creative Power of **Mind**, to recognize and remedy her self-sabotaging thoughts. Within months, she was offered two promotions that positioned her to impact the success and well-being of the female engineers in her company.

Freshly promoted to a director position, a promising young woman was suddenly plagued with "imposter" anxiety. At a time when she needed to be visible and directional she held back. Through the Co-Creative Power of **Feelings** she realized that her boss's critical style was triggering feelings of unworthiness that she had taken on from her mother. By excavating that untruth she was able to banish those feelings and rise to the challenge. Her subsequent recognitions and inspiring leadership resulted in her being showcased in her company's video about how women can advance.

A disgruntled senior executive with a Fortune 50 company was ready to give notice, until she realized that it was she who had stalled her career waiting for others to validate her and provide her with her next opportunity. Through the Spiral Up! process she became so practiced at the Co-Creative Power of **Speech** that she was able to purposefully articulate her value to herself and others. The result: she found her true calling right in her own company.

A manager at a Fortune 50 company began to feel perturbed that there were many women minorities in her company who seemed devastatingly unfulfilled and were not advancing in their careers. Working with the Spiral Up! principles and the Co-Creative Power of **Action**, rather than holding others responsible, she organized an internal Asian Women's professional group that helped them gain visibility and promotions. Her willingness to take a risk to support other women in rising has led to other important opportunities not just for herself in her professional and personal life but also for these other women. Since then, she has been presented with exciting opportunities inside and outside her company including invitations to join boards, and is more committed than ever to act boldly on behalf of less advantaged women.

The word *evolution* contains *volution*, a word meaning "one turn in the spiral." Laying claim to more of ourselves with each turn of our own spiral, we are brought closer to the wisdom and truth at our core. As we become more authentic, we rise higher in spiritual and personal power. As you learn how to trust life's unfolding and to savor what you have and who you are, you will discover a flow and rhythm to your life. You, too, will experience the passion and power that comes from living and working according to your own truths and feminine strengths.

So how do we get there?

The Three Turnings of the Spiral

Before entering the three Turnings of the Spiral, we all inhabit a level of consciousness experienced as a repetitive loop—life by default. This is the experience of sleepwalking through life, reacting to life's triggers from our patterns and programming. Identified with our ego self, we feel deep down that something is wrong—with the situation or, more likely, with us—and we set out to prove our worth. Our dominant motivator on what I call the linear, or horizontal, path is fear, which compels us to try to get something to make ourselves feel better, safe, or secure.

If we don't evolve past this dimension, we continue to make decisions and take actions based on our false self. This false self tries to make us believe that we are what we do, what people think of us, and what we have. But, in actuality, it is the number one way we lose power.

Never static, ever flowing, the Spiral Up! process shows us how to evolve from the false self to become our most powerful and loving selves. As we become more aware of how to work with the dynamism of the spiral, we learn to go through, not around, the tough stuff. We face into what is keeping us closed—beliefs, feelings, or circumstances of our lives—and transform them so that we become more alive and more purposefully engaged.

To transition from a *life by default* to an *inspired life*, we must keep our channel open and flowing. The spiral represents this revolution of renewal—a constantly evolving, fluid process of saying yes to what wants to be born in us and letting go of what is no longer relevant. As we learn to open and release what no longer fits, our authentic self is revealed, and with it, our true gifts.

Let's take a moment to examine these three turnings in more detail.

Initiation: The First Turning

We awaken from a life by default and enter the First Turning of the Spiral through what I call an initiation—often activated by a loss, heartbreak, illness, or melancholy, or simply by finding ourselves in uncharted waters. At this point we have a choice to become fully responsible, conscious co-creators and authors of our lives. In the First Turning of the Spiral we learn ways to shift our identification from thoughts and feelings that make us suffer to a deeper, more genuine part of us that longs to open our hearts and enlighten our minds.

Aspiration: The Second Turning

The word that describes our innermost essence, our *spirit*, derives from the Latin word *spiritus*, meaning "breath," "air." We enter the Second Turning of the Spiral when we realize that beyond our egoic selves is an almighty, universal energy that is being "breathed" through us. We can experience this as a fierce longing to bring higher levels of truth, beauty, and goodness to the world. Here, at this Second Turning, we shift from "What's in it for me?" to "How can I become the best, most authentic version of myself?"

Inspiration: The Third Turning

The word *inspire* is defined as "to fill with an animating, quickening, or exalting influence." Inspiration isn't something we need to talk ourselves into—it just lifts us up. It is the creative principle expressed when we feel the rush of *I gotta do it!* It is a pregnant idea or feeling that enthusiastically prompts us to express our gifts. It is what lights us up and brings shine to our eyes. It urges us to answer the question, "How can I serve?"

Introducing the 5 Co-Creative Powers

The Spiral Up! journey is a discovery of the deepest dimensions of self. But it is the Co-Creative Powers that are the transformative inner workings of the spiral—the system by which we access and activate our inner power. Put another way, if the spiral is the road map, the Co-Creative Powers are the engine that propels us.

We were designed to be co-creators. We live in a participative universe. All day long, and in every moment, through our energy, thoughts, feelings, words, and actions, we co-create our reality and shape the world around us. The trouble is, we mostly create out of patterns and conditioning that we're not even aware of. We have ambition, but we don't have the "power" tools to connect that ambition with what has meaning for us so that we can realize our dreams and offer up our gifts. Our five Co-Creative Powers—our inherent capacities to co-create—often lie dormant.

At each of the three turnings, *Spiraling Upward* works by helping you awaken latent capacities and turn them into Co-Creative Powers—of Energy, Mind, Feelings, Speech, and Action—so that they can become powerful portals to expressing yourself fully in the world. And here's the amazing part: when you become skillful with your Co-Creative Powers, there's almost nothing you can't achieve in life, and not from a pushy or grabby place but from a place of ease and grace. Anchored in your authentic self, your desire for achievement for achievement's sake falls by the wayside as you begin to make a difference wherever you go. You naturally step into your power, purpose, and place in the world.

When you bring your whole self to a conversation, or refrain from reacting in the moment, or shift your energy state, or neutralize a negative thought, you are using your Co-Creative Powers to evolve and uplift yourself and those around you. These may seem like simple things but they're not. They are the means to our powerful reinvention—our human tool kit for self-evolution.

---

5 Co-Creative Powers

The Co-Creative Power of Energy

What energetic message are you sending right now? Your external reality is *always* a reflection of your energy, or internal state. In default mode your energy might feel heavy, scattered, stagnant. Learning to consciously express your energy in alignment with the impact or influence you intend is the first step in your journey of transformation.

The Co-Creative Power of Mind

Because we can only take actions consistent with *who* we think we are and *what* we believe, our thoughts determine the course of our lives. In default mode, your mind might take you through endless loops of worry, self-criticism, or blame. As we learn to let go of thoughts that no longer serve us and dwell on heightened possibilities, we become a conduit for joy, love, and creative contribution.

The Co-Creative Power of Feelings

A single negative experience has an impact equivalent to ten positive ones. No wonder we worry about what might go wrong! The Co-Creative Power of Feelings frees us from reacting to entrenched fears and hurts. As we learn to become intimate with our feelings, without being seized by them, we are naturally guided to claim the richness of each moment.

The Co-Creative Power of Speech

The words we use, just like our energy, thoughts, and feelings, are creative forces. Our words shape reality. In default mode you might find yourself gossiping, complaining, or withholding your truth. By employing the Co-Creative Power of Speech you learn how to use language not only descriptively but inventively, so that you communicate in ways that create more freedom and possibility.

The Co-Creative Power of Action

In default mode you may tend to procrastinate on what's really important—or you may barrel through life taking lots of actions that are not in service to what really matters. Deep inside we've each made a promise to live true to our potential. When you act in alignment with the divine spark within, life flows and synchronicity happens: right time, right place, right partners.

How to Use This Book

You probably already sense that reading this book will not be a spectator sport! The exercises that close each chapter are designed to inspire the kind of inner-directed change you can usually get only when working one on one with a coach. Here's your part—you'll need to reallocate a portion of your attention and intention from wherever it goes now to what really matters to you by engaging with the concepts and applying them to your own life. But just imagine what your life will be like if you put even one-quarter of the effort that you invest in your work into realizing your greater potential.

Transformation doesn't require months in a cave or on a mountaintop; it happens over time by mindfully engaging in the life that is in front of us. It's not an overnight process but the result of building congruency between our heartfelt intentions and our thoughts, words, feelings, and actions on a daily basis. We need to learn to walk our talk, boldly, passionately, and respectfully, as the divine selves that we are. To gain the most out of *Spiraling Upward,* you'll want to get yourself a special journal where you can answer the questions that I pose to you along the way. And remember, even after completing it, you can come back to this book as many times as you like. Each time you do, the Spiral Up! process will provide a richer and deeper journey.

I can tell you firsthand that if you engage this process, you will see dramatic positive changes in your life. I have seen it work with multitudes of women over many years. I share some of their stories along with my own, so that you can see your own path reflected in the voices of many. To protect the confidentiality of those who wish to remain anonymous, I have sometimes changed names and identifying characteristics such as profession or location, and in a few cases I have combined storylines to create a composite. The stories, however, remain a genuine reflection of the extraordinary transformations that took place.

Above all, honor yourself by following your own rhythm and pace to birth the new you. If you like, share your insights and discoveries with friends, and revel in the small and larger changes that begin to take place in your life. Every one of us has knowledge, skills, ideas, creativity, and wisdom to share—and at this moment in history, more of us than ever are ready to rise to power with the gifts we bring. My aim will be satisfied if *Spiraling Upward* emboldens you to let your true nature shine a bit brighter, bringing to life that irreplaceable gift of you. As one client shared, "After working with Wendy's process for six months, I see, speak, and act in ways that are more authentic, compassionate, and truly powerful. I stay grounded in the positive aspects of who I am and what I bring to the world. Today, I am empowered to create my life afresh, in every moment."

Are you ready to get started?

Where Do You Fall on the Evolutionary Path?

We are in the midst of a monumental shift in consciousness and culture. Each of us is being invited to wake up to our true purpose, cultivate our gifts, and live in alignment with our hearts. Where are you in your own transformational shift? Because we live in an interconnected universe, each and every time you evolve your thinking and behaviors even a little bit you shift the whole world.

On a scale of 1 to 5, with 1 being the mind-set in the left column ("Old Paradigm") and 5 being the mind-set in the right column (Spiral Up! Paradigm), assess the basis for your thoughts and actions. Be honest and nonjudgmental.

Old Paradigm		Spiral Up! Paradigm
Fear	1 – 2 – 3 – 4 – 5	Faith
Material success and status	1 – 2 – 3 – 4 – 5	Significance: making a difference
Scarcity: opportunities, fun, love, money, recognition, time	1 – 2 – 3 – 4 – 5	Sufficiency: grateful for all I have
Impressing others	1 – 2 – 3 – 4 – 5	Doing what brings me joy
Needing to "get"	1 – 2 – 3 – 4 – 5	Desiring to create and give true gifts
Being "good" or "nice"	1 – 2 – 3 – 4 – 5	Being authentic
Priority on security, comfort, safety	1 – 2 – 3 – 4 – 5	Priority on evolving, connection, contribution
Doubting myself	1 – 2 – 3 – 4 – 5	Being my own best advocate
Waiting for "someday"	1 – 2 – 3 – 4 – 5	Starting where I am right now
Me, me, me	1 – 2 – 3 – 4 – 5	Realizing we're all in this together

You can return to check in with your evolutionary path at any time during your journey.

You and you alone choose moment by moment who and how you want to be.

—Dr. Jill Bolte Taylor

The First Turning

Initiation

Initiation is the frequently unbidden—and sometimes inexplicable—impulse to escape the confines of our current existence and lay claim to our greater potential. We may experience it this way: we wake up one morning feeling either too comfortable or complacent or depressed, with a sense things are too dry and too dead, or craving more air—more aliveness. Or something unexpected may happen that radically changes everything. Either way, we come to realize that we must let go of the familiar if we are to open to what's calling.

We are built for change—literally. It has been scientifically established that cells inside the body constantly regenerate—brain cells every sixty days, stomach lining cells in three days, eye cells in less than forty-eight hours. Everything in our bodies is always changing—self-healing mechanisms are constantly at work. Our true self desires to follow this same evolution. Longing to experience higher levels of who we are—more happiness, more power, more authenticity—gives us the impetus to do the inner work necessary to discover our deepest purpose.

Initiation is no small thing. It's about embarking on a journey of profound transformation. As transformational expert Claire Zammit says in her Feminine Power telecourse, "The caterpillar, after all, isn't just looking for self-improvement, a better job, or improved communication skills; she actually creates a container in which she lets go of who she knows herself to be." Initiation is a big deal—and it can seem scary without a step-by-step process to help you on your way.

A guy I had a crush on in grade school called me a few years back, saying that he hated his job and felt stalled in his career. He explained that he knew deep down that if he just changed jobs, he'd soon find himself in the same rut. "There's something in me that needs to be reengineered," he mused. He was no longer willing to simply "rearrange deck chairs" when it felt like his life was sinking—he wanted real happiness and fulfillment. In fact, our conversation spurred me on to finish this book because in it I offer a methodology for that deep reengineering—by giving us access to our Co-Creative Powers. These are the most potent tools of transformation we have. They allow us to refashion our lives from the inside out. And as you begin your initiation—the starting place of a conscious life—you will activate the Co-Creative Powers that have lain dormant in you.

Right now, you may be longing to know what the next iteration of "you" will look like, what function it will serve, how you will make money, when you will see your vision more clearly. But don't worry about the details right now. You don't have to know what you are doing. All that's needed is trust that something within you does know what to do. You are pregnant with a seed of creation that is as unique to you as your fingerprints—original to only you and yet with a life of its own. Your job as a co-creator is to nurture this seed in you and continue to open to the truth of who you are, which is wanted and needed in the world.

CHAPTER 3

Take Charge of Your Energy

The Co-Creative Power of Energy

With his famous equation E=mc², Albert Einstein proved that when you come right down to it everything in the universe is energy. Both the physical plane of our reality of matter and the abstract reality of our mind are made up of energy patterns.

—Deepak Chopra

Everything depends on energy. Growing up, I experienced the confusing disconnect between what people said and what was really going on in their energy. To avoid being ambushed by others' unpredictable energy, I got really good at reading signals. But it was the wily disease of lupus that turned me into an energy expert. Because of my chronic fatigue, I had to learn exactly which experiences, feelings, food, activities, and thoughts contributed to or drained my energy. It was imperative that I pay close attention to what my body and mind needed in order to optimize the limited energy I had. Later, I was able to compassionately reflect back to the women I worked with the messages they were missing from their energy.

Everything is made up of energy—from our physical bodies to the words on this page to the thoughts you are thinking to the music that streams through a room. Like radio stations sending and receiving signals, we are constantly generating and receiving energy. Because of the Law of Attraction, the principle of "like attracts like"—we draw to ourselves experiences and encounters that match our energy.

When we are living by default, however, we don't control the energy we generate; we just receive whatever it happens to attract, then wonder why certain things happen or don't happen in our lives. Energy is vibration in the literal and physical as well as the esoteric sense. As we start to live more consciously, we positively activate the Co-Creative Power of Energy by learning to raise our frequency and direct it so that it is consistent with the vibration of our higher self and what we *want more of.*

Your energy affects your thoughts; your thoughts influence your feelings; your feelings color your words; and your words give rise to actions. Energy is the raw material that fuels everything else. And because it operates as the current behind all the other Co-Creative Powers—mind, feelings, speech, and action—energy is the first stop on our journey to transformation. As you will learn, as you travel through each Co-Creative Power, when you activate one the others reverberate. For instance, when you think, feel, speak, or act in ways that enliven you, you boost both the quantity and the quality of your energy. When you align your thoughts, words, feelings, and actions with positive, flowing energy, you become a magnet for good.

Research suggests that more than 70 percent of communication occurs without people having to say a single word. If someone is being arrogant or uninterested, no matter what she says, we feel put off. When we interact with a person who is warm and kind, even if he isn't perfectly eloquent, we are drawn in.

We read people's energy, whether or not we're aware of it, just from the way they walk into the room. Think of the energy that emanates from the guy who ambles into a room, shoulders rolled forward, head down—do we gravitate toward him? Do we even notice the mousy woman with apologetic energy who seems to disappear as she slips in the door?

Being Versus Doing

Energy, or who we are being, is the context for everything else in our lives, the first force behind everything we think, feel, say, or do. And yet, when we think about changing things up, we usually resolve to *do* something different; we might read self-help books, take seminars, lose weight, revamp our résumé, possibly even consider a nip and tuck. We take *action.* Actions, of course, are crucial to changing our lives, but if we aren't addressing the context within which all actions take place, we create superficial change, not transformation.

When we bypass our energy and rush into action, our efforts can even backfire. Say you want to be more recognized and rewarded at work but fear that you will fall short compared with your coworkers. Perhaps you also think that your boss is not looking out for your best interests. Without knowing it, the actions you take, whether these are speaking up in meetings, offering to take on special projects, or even holding casual conversations with workmates, will be tainted with fear and distrust and will attract more of the same. Your energy will tell on you.

Or if you think you're out of shape, you may decide you'll jump-start your health with a juice fast. If your energy is laced with punitive self-judgment, your fast could easily end up in a rebellious fall from grace, straight into a bag of chips.

Recall a time when you felt depressed or downhearted—this is not the best day to go for a job interview or call that guy who gave you his number. When our energy is low, we perceive "lack" within and around us, and it translates into feelings and thoughts of scarcity: we may feel needy, victimized, or helpless instead of self-sufficient, positive, and effective. Everything is affected by our energy, or *who we're being*, which is why it is essential to learn to shape this internal state with intention.

We have storehouses of this valuable resource within us, but we sometimes think that joy, enthusiasm, or even a cheerful mood happens purely by accident. We call on the Co-Creative Power of Energy as we learn to summon radiant, loving, and magnetic energy on demand.

Opening the Channel

Reality is extraordinarily fluid, constantly changing, mutating, and evolving. When we feel energy streaming through us we are living as spirit—our core essence. It's only when we've pinched off that flow that we cut ourselves off from our current of well-being. To flow spontaneously and effortlessly, we have to be aware of, and steer away from, thoughts and experiences that are energetically heavy or dense, and move instead toward thoughts that make us feel emotionally fluid and light.

When the energy channels of our spiral are open, we are more available to experience miracles. We tune in to subtle messages and transmit our intentions to the universe without static or interference. Flowing energy leads us to exude confidence and primes the rest of our Co-Creative Powers.

To create a juicy future that is beyond anything you've yet experienced, your energy *must* be flowing in this way. Dancing, running, laughing, and sex are just some of the activities that return us to our most fluid selves. You've probably experienced this phenomenon yourself thousands of times through the mood-lifting benefits of exercise. Whenever I swim, practice yoga, or dance, I notice a breakthrough moment when my bound-up energy is freed to flow again. At those times I feel as though I could go on forever. Afterward, I'm more optimistic, carefree, spontaneous, and resilient; whatever I do next is enhanced with expanded possibilities.

Contemplative practices are also effective energy shifters. You can do a complete turnaround in your energy and your day simply by taking five minutes to sit quietly and deepen your breathing. In each Turning of the Spiral, you will discover new and different ways to free the flow of your energy.

Energy Checkup

Reflect upon each of these questions, and answer them on the continuum of "mostly," "sometimes," "rarely," or "never."

Are you aware of the energy you emit?
Are you aware of the impact your energy has on others?
Do you think of your energy as an asset that draws positive situations and people to you?
Are you aware of others' energy?
How often do you consciously shift and uplift your energy?

Take a moment right now and lift your energy or mood from wherever it is to a little bit higher place. You can do it! Once you do, notice what is possible that wasn't possible before.

We do not attract that which we want, but that which we are.

—James Allen

Conscious Energy

Although we do not typically wake up in the morning and ask, "Who shall I create myself to be today?," in a very real sense, this is what we do. We are intentional human beings, and we have a choice about what we create. Every situation offers us a new opportunity to become more conscious of our role as co-creators. The substance of what we create comes not from *what* we do but from *how* we do it—the quality of our energy.

When we become intentional with our energy, or who we are being, we take care to offer genuinely warm, positive energy. By consciously authoring our energy so that it's in alignment with our spirit, we are more trusting, accepting, courageous, and open. And because what we put out comes back to us, the degree to which we are deliberate about our energy, or who we are being, is the degree to which we experience personal power, "good luck," and even miracles.

Our energy is like the sound track that plays behind the movie of our lives. It can be as calm and hypnotic as a majestic symphony, as threatening as the score for *Jaws*, or as jubilant as a marching band in a Fourth of July parade.

Since our predominant energy state is what our life reflects back to us, it is critical to be conscious of the flavor of energy we emanate. The more enthusiastic, loving, and open we are, the faster energy flows through us, the higher our "vibrational frequency," and consequently the more wonderful the gifts we attract. We evolve by tuning in to our energetic melody and by taking responsibility for raising it.

A surefire way to access the Co-Creative Power of Energy is by intentionally embodying *a way of being*. About twenty years ago, some girlfriends and I were returning from a personal retreat. As we said our good-byes at the airport, we each took a moment to declare who we would *be* that year. We each selected three or four words that would set the tone for the energy we wanted to exude over the next twelve months. The words I selected were so outrageous they were almost intimidating: extraordinary, magnanimous, influential, and playful. I thought, "I live in a tiny studio apartment. I have five clients. Who do I think I am?" But these were qualities of energy that called to me, and they inspired me to grow.

And that year some amazing things happened. *Fortune* magazine called to interview me for an article on coaching. It was the first time I had ever been quoted as an expert in a publication. Next, I was invited to be a "Champion of Hope" by the National Kidney Foundation. This award was given annually to three kidney transplant recipients who had achieved success in the world.

On the night of the fundraiser, as I stepped up to the microphone to share my story, I looked out at the gleaming faces of supporters, including five tables of friends who had come to celebrate with me. I offhandedly shared a funny anecdote about the doctor who was being honored with us and made everyone laugh. I realized how, without my even thinking about it, the universe had served up an opportunity for me to practice being extraordinary, magnanimous, influential, and playful all at once!

If you become masterful with only one Co-Creative Power—your energy—this will begin to transform you into the woman you were always meant to be. In the following sections, you will learn new ways to consciously open and free your energy as well as deliberately direct it. In doing so, you'll discover firsthand the incredible capacity of your internal state to open you up to the work of the divine—your highest guidance.

Looking Ahead

In the rest of this chapter, you will be coached to recognize your own energy patterns, including negative ones, and you'll learn methods to redirect your energy to Spiral Up. You will see how, by embodying a way of being, you will:

- Learn to attract more of what you want
- Take charge of your energy
- Deposit energy in your energy bank account
- Discover the joy of living from your essence

Stories

Like the wind, energy is made visible by the impact it has. Read on to see how a work relationship fraught with anger and retaliation helped one client come to terms with—and transform—an unconscious and aggressive energy pattern.

Rebecca's Story: The Samurai

Rebecca, a corporate vice president, wanted to shed what she called her "adversarial, fear-based energy." But at the time I first coached her, that energy was somewhat ingrained. In a troubling and recurring situation, another VP, Brenda, was constantly disagreeing with Rebecca's decisions and gossiping to others about her. Rebecca fretted, "I know she's spreading rumors all over the department that it's me who's at fault. It's damaging!" Rebecca's aggressive energy had found a match in Brenda's; they were in a destructive loop.

Before her career in business, Rebecca had been a teacher of a mutinous class of seventh graders who'd driven the two previous teachers to quit. Rebecca was young, but she learned quickly how to hold her ground by giving a look that could silence the room.

Later, as a woman in a male-dominated workforce, she often felt walked over. But she was proud of her ability to stick up for herself, a trait that gradually escalated into an unconscious habit of annihilating people with witty criticism. This aggressive energy pattern was a survival strategy for Rebecca. It was also a huge deterrent to the emergence of her more authentic, powerful, wise, and loving self.

Rebecca had a porcelain statue of a samurai warrior in her office that stood on a bookshelf behind her desk. The samurai represented Rebecca's approach to life—defensive and at the ready, often making preemptive strikes to protect her more vulnerable self. Because of her own insecurities about being powerful, however, she saw the samurai as the stereotypical aggressive warrior.

Out of curiosity, I did some research on the samurai's honorable traditions. I discovered that there was another side to the samurai—an energy much deeper than aggression—to explain the samurai's motivations. The samurai valued courage, loyalty, honor, friendship, sincerity, and compassion. They were passionately committed to removing any obstacles in the way of living authentically. And although the word *samurai* means "warrior," it also means "to serve."

As we worked on identifying who Rebecca wanted to be, we found that the energy qualities she desired lined up perfectly with the samurai's noble values. Seeing this inspired Rebecca to let go of the aggressive energy style she had once depended on for survival. Parting with her old combative energy took immense courage, but the old energy pattern was counterproductive to her higher desire to live from her values and purpose.

One day I asked Rebecca, "Who are you committed to being? Do you want to be known as a person who can win a fight?" Rebecca's energy shifted instantly. "No," she replied. While Rebecca did not want to lose her edge, she, like the samurai, had a deeper desire within—to serve the greater good. Rebecca learned to withdraw her attention from Brenda, and in every interaction with coworkers she practiced her commitment to being more caring and supportive. Employees began to seek her out for mentoring, and in a short time she received feedback from two executives that her counsel was immensely valued.

Brenda was the first to reach out. They never resolved any particular conflict, but because Rebecca had shifted her energy, there was no longer a provocation for Brenda to react to. Becoming close friends is probably not in their future, but the gossiping stopped and a workable relationship ensued.

Bonnie's Story: The Inner Vow

Bonnie was a well-respected leader who was known for her ability to get the job done. But even on weekends she was perpetually in motion. Moving from one task to the next, she dutifully followed the voice in her head that impatiently insisted that she be productive. She was like many of us in our productivity-centric culture. Without some awareness, it's all too easy for us to define ourselves solely by a self-imposed meritocracy of "What have you accomplished lately?" Instead of thoughtfully attending to what's important, we reactively chase after whatever seems urgent in the moment.

One weekend Bonnie's seven-year-old daughter, Cherie, pranced into the living room in her sparkly pink fairy dress and spun around exclaiming, "Mommy, watch me dance!" Bonnie gave her a perfunctory "Yes, honey." But Cherie's radiant face didn't even register in Bonnie's mind until she was walking away toward another task. It suddenly struck her how many times she had brushed off Cherie in favor of her to-do list.

Bonnie shared this story with me in response to our coaching inquiries "Who do you want to be?" and "What do you want to be known for?" Her fresh realization from the previous weekend still stung. Knowing who she *didn't* want to be helped her clarify who she *did* want to be, not just at home but at work and in the world.

I introduced Bonnie to a powerful alignment tool I call the Inner Vow. It is one of the most effective coaching tools I've ever used because it expands the context in which we approach life by reminding us to align with our highest vision of ourselves. An Inner Vow is made up of your values, purpose, and who you are committed to being. It serves as a compass that guides you to live true to who you really are.

When Bonnie created her Inner Vow, she made sure to prioritize her commitment to slow down and savor what was truly important. Bonnie's vow connects her head with her heart, freeing her to move away from continual busyness to a more centered energy that enables her to be present to what truly matters and has meaning.

This is what she wrote:

Who I am in the world is an authentic, loving woman committed to living with passion and integrity. I enjoy life and relax into each moment. I bring understanding and unconditional presence to every interaction and moment.

Women's work is always toward wholeness.
                                                    —May Sarton

Exercises

Your Inner Vow: Decree Who You Will Be

The act of making an Inner Vow is your personal commitment to a way of being or identity that will permeate every action you take and shape the results you produce. As Bonnie learned, by declaring who you will be, you establish inner authority—an inner locus of control, a ground of being from which everything else in your life springs. Our purpose in life is less about what we do than how we do it. Your Inner Vow will provide you with the context for how you think, feel, speak, act, and attract.

In the following sections you will identify your values and who you want to be, the two ingredients necessary for your Inner Vow. By referring to your vow regularly, just as you might receive regular chiropractic adjustments, you will be supported in standing tall for the truth of who you are.

1. **Values.** True integrity is living your values, purpose, and potential. Your values are heartfelt beliefs and ambitions for how you want to live your life. As you deliberately define your values or credo, you will be inspired to live true to your higher self. When you live true to yourself, you don't hide your light—you shine! You express yourself and your gifts in the quirky, quiet, or sometimes outrageous ways that are uniquely and naturally you.

When you do what is authentically yours to do, you feel good about yourself, which attracts more good into your life. When you live from integrity—which is the very best of you—magic happens. The universe conspires to fulfill your heart's desires.

Name three people who have touched or inspired you. Examples: Maya Angelou, my mother, Angelina Jolie, Jane Goodall.

What is it about these people that inspires you? What values do they embody that most attract you? Example: Jane Goodall might represent for you a sense of mission or adventure. Identify what you are drawn to in the person to determine one of your values.

Before we move on to the second stage of this exercise, it's important to understand the relationship between a value and a quality of being. The latter represents the embodiment of a value. Thus, a value of adventure might translate as *being* playful, risk-taking, or curious. A value of fairness, for example, might translate as *being* inclusive, empathetic, or even-handed.

2. Qualities of being. Identify three qualities of being that most call to you. Select words that inspire and stretch you, not merely those that describe your current self. You will weave your chosen qualities together with your values to create your Inner Vow.

Examples of *being* words: Outrageous, unstoppable, peaceful, playful, generous.

3. Create Your Inner Vow. An Inner Vow is a promise to yourself and the world. It will serve as a reminder to you to bravely live by your true values, treat yourself and others in a certain way, and live your potential. It is not a description of you now, but a pointer to who you are becoming. Your Inner Vow should be two sizes too big, like clothes you are growing into. Craft it in such a way that when you read it you feel a sense of excitement—what I call a "giddy-up" feeling!

Take your answers from the above exercises and create your Inner Vow:

Who I am is a _____, _____, _____ (quality of being words) woman committed to living by _____, _____ (values words) in the world.

Here are some examples, written by women in my Spiral Up! workshops. Let them inspire you as you write your own vow.

Who I am is an affectionate, loving woman and a charismatic leader who courageously follows my own truth.

Who I am is a force for positive change inspiring others to greatness through continually expressing humility, kindness, understanding, and personal integrity.

Who I am is an extraordinary, playful woman who is committed to full self-expression, bold authenticity, and living life fully from the heart.

Feel free to edit or rearrange the words in your own Inner Vow or add a sentence until it feels right. Flexibility and authenticity are integral to the Spiral Up! path—so make this statement your own. That way, it will serve as your touchstone and inspire you to live from your most authentic self.

Inner Vow Practice

Write down your Inner Vow and post it where you'll see it every day. You can place it on your bathroom mirror, copy and paste it into your digital calendar so that it pops up first thing every morning, put it in a frame on your desk or bedside table, or create an inspiring screen saver.

Read it daily, and every time you do, let it permeate you until you feel it *as you*. Refer to it before important interactions or meetings and ask yourself, "How would I speak or act if I were fully embodying my Inner Vow right now?"

> **Commitment is what transforms a promise into reality. It is the words that speak boldly of your intentions… the actions that speak louder than words. It is the daily triumph of integrity over skepticism.**
>
> **—Anonymous**

Fill Your Energy Bank Account

Too much stress zaps energy. In the fight-or-flight response, our diaphragms tighten, our heart rate goes up, and our bodies pump out harmful stress hormones like cortisol and epinephrine. Handy, if we actually need to fight or flee, but they cause physiological damage if secreted on a habitual basis. Equally important, when our energy state is tightly wound we have zero access to our intuition and wisdom.

Fortunately for us, women have a broader behavioral repertoire under pressure than just "fight or flight." Under stress we also "tend and befriend." Researchers have discovered that as part of our stress response, we release the hormone oxytocin, which encourages us to tend to children and gather with other women. As we do, more of the bonding hormone is released, producing a calming effect. Simply by talking with or seeing friends, we experience a positive and quantifiable shift in our energy.

Filling your energy bank account is often more about what you don't do than what you do. It's amazing what can happen when we abstain from energy-zapping activities and when we get enough sleep, the right nutrition, and some "me" time. What creative solutions have you discovered to keep your energy account balanced and full? Reflect on the ways you make "deposits" into your energy account—these might include seeing friends, reading, exercising, or taking a bath. What depletes your energy account? Negative self-talk, working too much, worrying, and watching too much TV are common culprits—be aware of the behaviors that drain you and commit to curtailing them.

Which of my energy deposits will I commit to doing more of this week?
Which of my energy withdrawals will I abstain from doing this week?

Dead or Alive Energy

Keep a running tally: on a piece of paper, draw a line down the center of the page. At the top of the left column put a minus sign (–) and at the top of the right column put a plus sign (+). Throughout the day, jot down the activities that deplete your energy and those that infuse you with vitality.

What experiences or interactions most brought me alive today?
What definitely did not bring me alive?

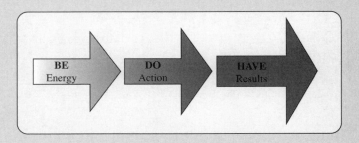

Highlights

- The circumstances of our lives reflect our predominant internal state—our energy.
- Rebecca's story illustrates a simple way to shift combative energy.
- Bonnie's story reveals how you can shift your energy by committing to a new way of *being*.
- By recognizing our energy ruts—well-grooved, automatic *energetic* reactions—we can change them.
- To be happy and healthy we must make more energy deposits than withdrawals.

Use some or all of the following questions to help you affirm or remember what resonated most with you in this chapter.

What qualities of energy are you transmitting when you are on automatic?

What benefits have you noticed when you exude the energy that you most want to be?

What is one deposit you will make in your energy account tomorrow?

CHAPTER 4

Author Your Thoughts

The Co-Creative Power of Mind

The moment you start watching the thinker, a higher level of consciousness gets activated.
—Eckhart Tolle

After years of struggling with lupus, the disease took its toll. My kidneys began to fail and I had to undergo dialysis while waiting for a donor. Because no one in my family was able to donate a kidney, I knew the chances of receiving a match that my body would accept were very low. It was hard to imagine a rosy future.

Yet I knew that my very survival depended on being able to hold a higher intention than circumstances imposed. My lifeline was the daily practice of letting go of negative thoughts, and replacing them with thoughts that were more uplifting. It was not an easy or quick process. On the other hand, the waiting list for kidneys was long, giving me plenty of time to practice.

If I started to feel defeated, I would interrupt the fears from taking me on a downward spiral and remind myself that there was a bigger plan for me. I firmly believed that I was here for a purpose. I had much to do and couldn't afford to entertain depressing thoughts. By the time that miraculous phone call came telling me they had found a kidney that was my perfect match, I was ready to receive the grace of that moment.

You've just been introduced to energy—the first Co-Creative Power. You may already be noticing small or even significant changes in your mood or energy state. Now we'll take this next step of our journey together as I show you how to use the Co-Creative Power of Mind.

Your energy and your thoughts are in constant two-way communication. Your energy, or "vibe," shapes the quality of your thoughts. Likewise, your thoughts color your energy or mood. In fact, what we think about most often lays the path to our destiny. As you are about to learn, the Co-Creative Power of Mind creates the narrative thread of your life.

Many of us believe that we are what we think. It's easy to see why. All day long our minds talk to us. It's as if we have an endless radio "Thought Show" going on in our heads, and because it's our 24–7 companion, we eventually come to think of our thoughts as who we are. This is how it is when we live by default: we can get so caught up in our thoughts that they lead us around like a dog sniffing at everything along its path.

The point is not to turn off the radio—it wouldn't be possible anyway—but we do need to change the channel. Psychologists tell us that we think an average of sixty thousand to eighty thousand thoughts a day, and that about 90 percent of them are repetitive and negative. The voice in our head is more often than not hypercritical, self-sabotaging, and a downright bully!

The spiral represents the principle of *as within, so without*: our most frequently played narratives—or thoughts—will sooner or later materialize in our lives. Whatever we're thinking circulates back to us, not just the goodwill, optimism, and love we intend, but also the worry, bitterness, or smallness we harbor. Beneath your negative thinking patterns, however, runs a deeper stream of your essence. That is the truth of who you are. You are an ever-shifting expression of a magnificent and unlimited ocean of potentiality; you are capable of so much more than you can ever imagine. No matter what has happened in your life so far, it doesn't have to define you.

Your Mind As Divine Headquarters

Every one of us has a deep desire to grow into who we really are—our whole, complete, and unlimited self. And every one of us has immense interior resources to live our unique purpose. The ancient Greeks called it our inner spirit, or *daimon*, the genius of our soul. If you are sensing a desire to express yourself at a new level, that is your *daimon* nudging you to rise to your power and grow into your potential. To evolve, we must stop looking outside of ourselves, quiet our minds, and tune in to the wisdom of our daimon—our inner authority.

From this place, our thoughts don't run us any more. By compassionately greeting, questioning, and turning around thought chains that we used to blindly believe and follow, we train our focus on our highest good. This is how we exercise our ability to choose joy, love, and goodness in every moment.

The ancient Greeks pictured the *daimon* as a golden figurine that would be revealed by chipping away an exterior layer of cheap ceramic (one's superficial self). This is our journey of Spiraling Up: the revealing of what's already true about us, the unveiling of our essence. Our task is to peel back beliefs of separation, smallness, and unworthiness and come into the full expression of our golden selves.

Moment to moment, we can choose to identify with this expansive self—the generous, wise, spiritual "I" who knows everything is going to work out. This is very different from listening to the "ticker tape" of the fearful, small, oft-complaining voice in our heads that scares the heck out of us with its catastrophic predictions. Even if it stays covered over for days, months, or years, we each have this deep well within where peace, passion, and wisdom live. The word *idea* has the Latin "dea" within it, meaning *deity* or *goddess*. When your mind is open and clear, it works like a satellite receiver for divine direction.

When we trust the messages from the universe and our own body, intuition, and feelings, we heed our inner authority—we listen to our *daimon*. Like writers selecting the words to use, we learn to govern our thoughts by receiving them without judgment, releasing those that don't serve us, and refocusing our minds on what brings us alive. We become artful editors of our internal stories. We reimagine our life as a heroine's tale deserving of respect and compassion, and we welcome challenge as part of creating an inspired life. This inner authority gives us authorship. We become the tellers of our own tale.

As you enter more deeply into The Co-Creative Power of Mind, you will learn the skills of receiving, releasing, and refocusing the mind to Spiral Up! You'll learn to let go of limiting thoughts and rewrite your inner script to create a new story—the one you were always meant to live.

Thoughts Checkup

Reflect upon each of these questions, and answer them on the continuum of "mostly," "sometimes," "rarely," or "never."

Are you aware of your ticker-tape thoughts?
Are you aware of what your mind is telling you?
Do you believe your thoughts are creating a positive narrative?
Are you aware of how your thoughts are impacting your destiny?
What would be possible if you took your negative thoughts less
    seriously?

See if you can shift from a negative thought to a more uplifting thought. Remember, it's all about practice!

When I'm trusting and being myself as fully as possible, everything in my life reflects this by falling into place easily, often miraculously.

—Shakti Gawain

From Autopilot to Conscious Creator

Everything that has been created in life began as a thought. We also establish who we are with our thinking. Who you think you are is who you will become, and that's why it is essential to shift your thinking from autopilot to conscious creation.

It is a common human misperception to feel somehow incomplete. Albert Einstein had a phrase for this kind of thing: *optical delusions.* Often buried in our subconscious, we each have a personalized version of this collective "lack story" supported by so-called evidence of our less-than-perfect selves.

This built-in thought pattern that tells us we need something or someone to complete us is fueled by a spiritual hunger that is meant to inspire us to wholeness. But instead of embarking on an inward journey to know our greater selves, most of us attempt to find our sense of worth in *doing* or *acquiring* more.

For many of us, the first thirty-five years or so are spent fulfilling an agenda that has been superimposed on us from the outside. Without knowing it, we embark in a direction that is driven by an underlying need to prove our worth and seek approval. Our hunger for A's—attention, acceptance, approval, and affluence—makes us grasp *outwardly*. We try to experience, acquire, or accomplish something that will, once and for all, make us think of ourselves as enough.

This obsession with external conditions often plays out by prioritizing everyone's needs above our own. We essentially abandon ourselves by thinking: What do they need? What do they think? What would make people respect or like me?

We don't have to believe what our thoughts tell us. If we relate only to the part of ourselves that is striving and stressed out, grasping and gnarled up in the worries of the day, we cut ourselves off from the spacious sky of our nature. We are each a perfect expression of our one source. That core part of you, call it soul, love, or spirit, never abandons you. This constant, wise source is unafraid. It knows you have already made it through tough times and become stronger because of them.

But when we let our automatic thoughts rule, just like a garden hose gets kinked, our mind gets tied up in knots—or, as I like to call them, kNOTs. A kNOT is a negation of ourselves, of our life. It takes conscious awareness and skill to first notice a kNOT and then untie it.

When you sit quietly and allow your thoughts to drift, you likely notice another kind of consciousness seeping through. This isn't a rarefied state reserved for experienced meditators. We all meditate, whether we call it that or not: in our gardens, riding a bike, or pleasurably stretched to the limits of doing what we love. In these grace-filled moments, time stops and a quiet but riveted inner presence becomes palpable. It is in these instances that your true self shows itself to be much deeper than the internal chitchat we're so used to listening to. In fact, your spirit—the real you—is listening to your mind.

Witnessing and Transforming

This realization that you are the *witness* of your thoughts (not your thoughts themselves) is the doorway to real freedom. Only when we know ourselves as distinct from our thoughts can we accept or discard whatever the mind delivers. By observing our thoughts impartially, we can pause between stimulus and response; we no longer must follow in blind obedience wherever our mind takes us. We can choose which thoughts deserve our energy.

The best-selling book *A Course in Miracles* says that, every moment, we're either extending love or projecting fear. Our thoughts are steering us either upward or downward. Most thoughts come from early programming that goes against who we are: "Don't say that! Don't do that! Don't eat like that! Don't look like that!" Without awareness, our minds run amok.

I experienced this powerfully at the height of my illness, when I needed high doses of a steroid medication that caused loss of appetite, mood swings, and insomnia. After weeks of very little sleep, I became scattered and forgetful. At the local theater one night, a panic came over me when I realized I couldn't follow a simple plot in a Charlie Brown play. My fear escalated the following day when I hopped on the scale and discovered I had lost fifteen pounds.

My mind became a whirlpool of worrisome thoughts. I blamed myself for the shape my life was in. As I swam laps in the local pool one day, the negative narrative played like a broken record in my mind: What do you have to show for your life? You don't have a family or a job. If you hadn't been so irresponsible you wouldn't have gotten sick in the first place!

Suddenly something shifted. I had just *witnessed* my verbal assault and realized that *I* was *listening to* the harsh voice. If *I* was listening to it, then maybe it wasn't *me*. I was at once stunned and relieved.

No matter what we have done in life, we are usually doing the best we can given what we know at the time. Deep down, I had always believed that we were made in the image and likeness of a beneficent source. It made sense that this all-knowing, wise, and compassionate energy would never speak to me in such a nasty way. For the first time it occurred to me that the cruel voice I was so often ruled by might not be right—and that I had it in my power to change the way my thoughts spoke to me by choosing to receive, release, and refocus them.

> **For him who has conquered the mind, the mind is the best of friends; but for one who has failed to do so, his mind will remain the greatest enemy.**
> **—The Bhagavad Gita**

Minding the Three R's

Buddhism, like most contemplative practices, aims to liberate us from our monkey minds so that we can experience the peace of who we really are. My way of approaching my own obsessive thinking builds on that premise by receiving, releasing, and refocusing my thoughts. **Receiving** is noticing and welcoming every thought. Since our thoughts aren't really *who* we are, we can take a step back and behold our own self-inflicted judgments as one of the qualities that make us all human. This is the first step in transforming our thoughts through awareness.

Second, we can **release**. Although our thoughts may sound very familiar, what we're thinking isn't necessarily true. Usually, our most commonly played grievance stories all have similar plotlines. Just the act of noticing our "tapes" can be freeing. Have some fun with this. As you do with old friends, you can have a playful exchange with your negative thoughts, letting them know that they don't have the power they used to have over you.

And lastly, we can choose to **refocus** on a kinder interpretation of the matter at hand, or just on something that makes us smile. To make this shift, I like taking on the countenance of a wise elder or a sweet mother who helps me compassionately reinterpret experiences in my favor.

Let's say, for example, that I have a crush on someone who shows no interest in me. It would be easy to spiral down on some thought like, "I knew it! He wasn't attracted to me. I must not be pretty enough." Instead, I can receive my negative thoughts by noticing what I'm thinking, release my negative thoughts by not believing them, and refocus my thoughts on the positive in the situation: "If he's not interested in me, he must not be right for me." It frees up my energy to be available to someone who is.

This takes work. At first, it's enough to simply be aware of any thoughts that attempt to spiral you down. Pay particular attention to thought patterns that may have been playing in your head for many years. Just the act of compassionately noticing them is transformative. Soon you'll be interrupting them and reminding yourself that they are not necessarily true. All it takes to begin turning it around is to be more committed to feeling good than to the negative thought.

As you work with the Co-Creative Power of Mind at each of the three turnings in this book, you'll become increasingly adept at this three-step process. Soon it will become natural to Spiral Up! to a higher thought level, one that serves your peace of mind and genuine happiness. Remember, it is up to us to write our story. By claiming our inner authority, we author our thoughts—and our lives.

Looking Ahead

In the rest of this chapter, you will practice releasing what no longer serves you, and refocusing on the positive. Remember to keep your Inner Vow in mind to propel you onward and upward in your day-to-day life.

By authoring your thoughts you will:

- Learn to see your thoughts as separate from who you really are
- Become intentional with your thoughts
- Claim your inner authority
- Move closer to your life purpose

Stories

Women are serial transitioners. We love to reinvent ourselves. However, if we don't integrate and celebrate past successes, as well as let go of any assumptions or beliefs about how we've failed, we won't take our lives to the next level. Equally important is to set our intentions for what we want to create next. The women in the following stories will show you how.

Melissa's Story: The Right to Shine

Melissa was ten when she participated in what the neighborhood kids called a mandatory "cut" game. One by one, the eight girls and boys stood in the center of the circle and listened to their friends critique them. When it was Melissa's turn, she realized they had planned this "game" specifically for her. Ever since she had won a part in the school play, her friends felt she was acting "too big for her britches" and they wanted to bring her down a notch. It worked. The criticisms they flung at her stuck, and for years she unconsciously believed that it was dangerous to be too confident and that she had no right to be. When her love of singing and performing coaxed her into the limelight, her persecuting thoughts would almost paralyze her. Her body would tremble and a scarlet rash would emerge on her chest and neck.

Preparing for a performance one day, Melissa started having the same old shrinking feeling and noticed the rash beginning to appear. She thought, "Enough! What is this rash trying to tell me?" She heard, "Never get too big for my britches. It's not safe to believe in myself." Her internalized beliefs had surfaced. Now that they were at the conscious level, she could debate their validity and produce evidence of why she had a right to shine.

Melissa knew deep down that she was good; in fact, people reminded her all the time that she was not only a good person but a talented one. She began to focus on how her gifts lit people up, which gave her the confidence to pursue her love of singing and performing. Melissa is now the lead singer in a popular local band. Her ability to receive her wisdom, release the old story, and *refocus* on what she wanted more of helped her become the passionate performer she is today.

It takes great courage to break with one's past history.
—Marion Woodman

Shannon's Story: The Power of Completion

Shannon had a dream of making a film about swing dancing. She pulled off what seemed the impossible by writing the script, raising money, and producing an independent film that resulted in a theatrical production, appearances in film festivals, and a DVD release. When the experience was over, though, Shannon fell into a slump. She couldn't think of what to do next; nothing excited her. We sat down together and did a Completion Exercise, a way to thoroughly take stock of all that she had undertaken and accomplished.

Shannon realized that she had been so focused on the fact that the movie hadn't made tons of money that she had overlooked the amazing result she actually had achieved. By working through the Completion Exercise, Shannon recognized that she had achieved her primary goal of sharing this wonderful story with thousands of people.

Once Shannon acknowledged and appreciated all the aspects of her remarkable feat, her mind no longer had to hold the incomplete file open. With newfound closure, she was inspired to begin something new. And that she did: she sold her house. She returned to her beloved city to restart her life. She met the love of her life and was married four months later. And, with her husband, she launched a new business marketing an amazing piece of software he had developed.

Just because we finish something doesn't mean it is complete. The word *complete* is defined as "made whole, nothing left out." If you recall the sudden ending of a relationship when there was much more left to say, you'll realize the difference between the end of something and being complete. To be complete means there is no regret, resentment, guilt, attachment, or blame about what came before. We feel 100 percent available to what's next and in touch with our integrity and wholeness.

In our overstimulated life, we rarely "complete" or fully digest experiences. And yet, until we take in life's moments entirely by acknowledging and appreciating them, the past piles up in the cache of our consciousness, saying, "Complete me! Complete me!" Assimilating our experience and acknowledging it as complete creates space for something new to come in.

Exercises

What would it look like if you lived true to yourself, to your deepest values and your highest purpose? Use the exercises that follow to connect with a greater intelligence that has grand plans for you—and let go of the obstacles that keep your light from shining.

Completion: Emptying the Bowl

A journey doesn't really begin until we've dealt with unfinished business from the past. As Shannon discovered, incomplete or "undigested" experiences drain our attention from the present and clog our receptivity to the new. Worse still, when we haven't fully let go of what came before, we often project it into the future and re-create the past.

Until your bowl is empty you cannot refill it. This exercise will help you to review and assimilate a phase you've just moved through, so that what remains is an empty, open space for something entirely new to come in. You will know that you are complete when the little voice saying, "Complete me!" is quiet and a sense of freedom, serenity, and acceptance prevails.

Please look back at a recent phase in your life—an event, a project, a relationship, a period of time—and answer the questions below as honestly as you can.

1. Regarding this last phase of your life, do you have any disappointments, anything you perceive as a failure?
2. Regarding this last phase of your life, do you have any regrets, anything you wish you had done differently?
3. Regarding this last phase of your life, do you have any resentments? However you answered the first three questions, see if you can forgive yourself or the other person now. If not, ask yourself if you would be willing to forgive or be forgiven. Allow spirit to aid in your forgiveness.

    Release any disappointments, perceived failures, regrets or resentments. All you have to do is be willing to let them go.
4. Regarding this last phase of your life, what are you pleased with or proud of? For each answer, take a moment to relish the good feelings it evokes.
5. Is there anything left to acknowledge or to let go in order to be complete with this last phase of your life?

When you have no more answers and you feel lighter, declare that phase of your life complete!

Receive, Release, and Refocus Your Thoughts

In the next two turnings of the Co-Creative Power of Mind, you will gain skills to help you receive, release, and refocus your thoughts with ever greater ease. If you'd like to get a head start, follow these simple steps to Spiral Up!:

1. Become aware of your thought patterns. Practice witnessing your thoughts from an impartial point of view.
2. If you find yourself disturbed by a thought, question its validity.
3. Refocus your thoughts on something you are grateful for.

Envision: The Divine's Highest Wish for You

There is a power greater than yourself that you can call on for a vision of your higher purpose. Your true self is in continuous connection with this infinite intelligence. But to hear it, you must attune to it.

Find a quiet place where you will not be disturbed. Sit in a relaxed position and close your eyes. Lengthen your breaths.

Ask the following questions with a welcoming attitude and give yourself time to receive whatever comes. The answer might arrive days later through an unexpected source such as something you read, a song you hear, a dream, or a conversation with a friend. If an answer comes right away, take a moment to write it in your journal.

1. What is the Divine's greatest idea for my life at this time?
2. Is there an image or metaphor that symbolizes this vision?
3. What is the feeling or Energy behind my vision?
4. Who do I need to become to realize my vision?
5. What must I let go of to realize my vision?
6. What is the first step to bringing my vision alive?

Highlights

- Whatever we're thinking—goodwill or bitterness—eventually circulates back to us.
- We each have a personalized version of the universal "lack story."
- A kNOT, or "lack story," causes us to contract—and we must learn to unwind it.
- Melissa's story shows us that we can receive, release, and refocus our thoughts.
- Your daimon, or inner spirit, is nudging you to grow into your potential.
- Shannon's "completion" experience helps her to close one door and open another.
- The divine has a plan for your life that you can tune in to.

CHAPTER 5

Awaken the Wisdom of Your Heart

The Co-Creative Power of Feelings

The whole thing, the most difficult thing, is to wake the heart. Somehow one has to learn to be able to live in the heart, to judge from the heart, as ordinarily as we live in mechanical mind and judge from that.
—Rodney Collin

I am not someone who wakes up in a cheery mood every day. Half the time I have to deliberately shift my thoughts to gratitude or possibility before I even get up. But having access to my emotions is a blessing that I didn't always have.

When I was growing up my mother was intensely emotional. Being able to freely express her emotions could have been the secret to her longevity—she lived to a robust eighty-eight. If something bothered her she raged, and did not care where we were or who bore the brunt of it.

In trying not to be like my mother, I suppressed the more messy, emotional, feminine side of my nature. People thought of me as "cool," and eventually I believed that of myself. I stuffed my feelings and got down to business, advancing faster than others my own age. What I did not realize was just how many feelings were bubbling beneath the surface.

My illness was a pressure cooker. On top of it, the medication I had to take amplified every emotion. I had to face my feelings and work with them or suffer from extreme and uncontrollable mood swings. I'd seen the harm my mother's unbridled emotions had caused; it was essential I find

a healthy way to express my own. It became crucial that I recognize feel-
ings as they arose, and not deny them. Like the goddess Persephone, who
descended into the underworld, I learned to descend into each emotion as
soon as I became aware of it, to not shy away from it, but to look deeper
into its core for that seed of wisdom.

With the knowledge you have gained from the chapters on energy and mind, you are now poised to take full advantage of the awesome Co-Creative Power of Feelings to create a juicy, authentic life.

Your feelings are a powerful guide that can lead you to your heart's desires. So how do we bring this incredible Co-Creative Power of Feelings fully on board? How do we wake the heart?

We intuitively associate feelings with the heart. We say, "Have a heart," meaning be compassionate, or "I had a change of heart" when our feelings shift, and "It was heartfelt" to convey sincerity or depth of feeling. As well, we remind one another to "follow your heart" because we intuitively sense that our hearts are intelligent—a belief that research confirms. It is a scientific fact that a large percentage of the heart's cells are neural cells, functioning similarly to the brain, making the heart a cognitive organ of perception.

Scientists have found that the heart sends and receives electromagnetic signals that we experience as emotional messages. These are processed in specific centers of the brain, in the same manner as the more common senses of sight and smell. Our "heart brain," or nervous system within the heart, enables the heart to remember, learn, and make decisions independent of the brain's cerebral cortex. This ability allows us to download stimulus directly through the heart, offering an intuitive comprehension of meaning without words.

To navigate in uncertain times we need to live as close to the truth as possible. Our ability to *feel* is a sixth sense that enables us to "know" something before we intellectually grasp it. When we are intimate with our hearts, we get answers to our questions: Is this the right way for me? How do I feel about this? Does this ring true? Is this what I need? Do I say this or that? Is there a deeper, more genuine emotion beneath this feeling? The heart is direct and honest. Although we never lose this precious capacity to perceive from the heart, our emotional perception weakens if we become overly dependent on our minds.

In your heart, you already know.

—Zen saying

Permission to Feel

In our mechanized, fast-paced world, feelings are often viewed as weaknesses. Our intuitive sensitivity is glossed over, especially when it takes the form of subtle feelings that allow us to sense things without apparent or logical cause: the tension in a room, an uneasiness about someone's behavior, the pull toward a certain place or path. But remaining open to our feelings, however faint, can be our greatest asset.

Feminine "feeling" strengths like inclusiveness, empathy, humility, relatedness, vulnerability, flexibility, compassion, and collaboration are increasingly in demand in this connected, global society and matrixed organizations. In fact, studies show those leadership strengths are more valued in today's workplace than the traditionally masculine leadership skills of aggressiveness, decisiveness, and expediency. With nearly one billion women set to enter the global economy in the next decade, organizations that don't attract, develop, and advance women leaders—with their inherent ability to connect with others through their feelings—will be left behind.

When we give ourselves permission to know what we really know, feel what we really feel, and say what we really mean, we not only feel free and alive but we express our natural leadership gifts and contribute the very best of us. By learning to let feelings in and out, without clinging to them or being gripped or dominated by them, we live a more authentic and fulfilled life. And although our culture might lead us to believe that feelings aren't important, the truth is that they are greatly valued in many contexts.

Even during a market downturn, there are certain things we won't give up—like movies. The publishing industry as a whole declines yet sales of romantic fiction increase. Why are these so sacred to us? Because we want to feel good—we want to open our hearts!

Standing in my kitchen one night I was drawn by the haunting music coming from the TV in the living room. The acclaimed trumpeter Chris Botti and violinist Lucia Micarelli were performing the evocative piece "Emmanuel." Afterward I learned that Botti quietly praised Micarelli after every performance with a number—eight, ten, fifteen—indicating how many people in the first few rows had been moved to tears. I added myself to the list.

When we're openhearted, we enjoy the wide spectrum of feelings available in life. We treasure what moves us, like moments of deep connection revealed by a telltale gasp or the quickening of our pulse. Yet not all feelings give us this sense of expansion—some make us want to shut down.

Feelings—*e-motions*—are simply *energy* that needs to move. Feelings are messy, rowdy, and fluid. As babies, when we're hurt, we howl and release the upset, then return rapidly to our natural state of curiosity and joy. And yet as adults we try and control our emotions, even though they exist beyond our rational mind.

The last time you found yourself capsized by an upset, did you scream, yell, and express your abhorrence of whatever indignity had befallen you? Or did you suppress your feelings and internalize the "pinch," allowing it to take up residence in your psyche, diminishing your love and your light? Every time we hold on to pain instead of feeling and releasing it, it eats away some of our aliveness. Over time, these painful moments shape our attitudes, affect our bodies, and eclipse our true, joyful nature.

Feeling "the Pinch"

Challenging times and unkempt emotions can serve us in untold ways. We live in a spiral world that provides us with experiences to catalyze our strengths and bring out our best. When emotional "pinches" to our flow erupt in the form of anxiety, anger, sadness, hostility, jealousy, or guilt, we are being invited to transform. Like alchemists who turn lead into gold, we can learn to use depression to lead us to hope, embarrassment to cultivate humility, and envy to uncover the truth about what we really want. And when properly grieved, the pain of rejection and loss can increase our capacity to love. Our ability to process these uncomfortable feelings makes us wiser and more translucent to the light, love, and authentic power at our core.

Buddhist teacher Sharon Salzberg counsels us to tease apart emotions as we would a musical chord to hear the different notes within. When a hungry coyote carried off my cherished cat, Comet, I was bereft. Engulfed at first in tears and sadness, I hardly noticed the notes of guilt submerged below my grief. Despite knowing that another cat had disappeared a few weeks before, I had given in to Comet's persistent mewing and let him out.

Over time, I was able to forgive myself and to find other notes—ones of love and courage. Comet had opened me to unconditional love, and that meant allowing him his free-roaming nature, even as I feared for his safety. As his name aptly conveyed, Comet's shining boldness was a luminous legacy I could forever treasure and emulate.

As we welcome and witness all of our feelings with an attitude of curiosity, we develop emotional resilience, the strength to recover from painful times, and the ability to bounce back from adversity. Only by learning to go through, not around, life's "pinches" do we increase our capacity to Spiral Up! Every triumph over fear, anger, and animosity strengthens our spiritual center and our ability to unabashedly express our purpose.

As you journey into the Co-Creative Power of Feelings, an increasing capacity for joy will be available to you. By learning to fully process and shape your feelings instead of being their passive victim, you let your energy flow freely and you become a magnet for what you truly want. Guided by your feelings, you learn to live more authentically. You begin to see how to transform even difficult emotions so that the love in you expands. By opening to the fluidity of feelings in your life, you increase your experience of connection, spontaneity, and enthusiasm. You simply feel more alive.

Feelings Checkup

Reflect upon each of these questions, and answer them on the continuum of "mostly," "sometimes," "rarely," or "never."

Are you aware of your feelings in the moment?
Do you embrace the gamut of emotions?
Are you guided by your feelings?
Do you hold your feelings loosely and fluidly?

Right now, take a deep breath and scan your body for a moment. What are you feeling and where does that feeling reside—your head, heart, solar plexus, belly? Now see if you can breathe into that feeling and let it flow through you, rather than attaching to it.

> **This being human is a guest house.**
> **Every morning a new arrival.**
> **A joy, a depression, a meanness,**
> **some momentary awareness comes**
> **as an unexpected visitor.**
> **Welcome and entertain them all!**
>
> **—Rumi**

Bringing Down the Walls

Who we are at our core is magnificent, pure love. Learning ways to Spiral Up! in order to speak and act from a feeling place of love, contribution, and connectedness is the central teaching of this Co-Creative Power. Just as the sun steadfastly shines behind a downpour, our love is ever present. Even when we're caught in a mental kNOT or an emotional storm, even when we're in the grip of fear, our love is only obscured.

Recently, I watched a television special about Puppies Behind Bars, an organization that trains inmates to raise puppies to become service dogs for the disabled. One disabled veteran, Sergeant Hill, received a trained dog, Frankie, to help him with his post-traumatic stress disorder, the signature injury for returning war vets. Sergeant Hill's dog became his lifeline, preventing him from being seized by paralyzing, incapacitating nightmares and flashbacks. When Hill touches Frankie, he is rescued from the terror his mind is reliving and returned to something happy, alive, and good—a being who loves him.

The dogs help the prisoners who train them, too. One life-sentenced inmate, transformed by his experience of giving back and by his relationship with an unconditionally loving puppy, wept openly as he said, "I always thought it was a sign of weakness to show emotion. This experience has given me the ability to love again. It's been dormant in me for so long because of the cold place that I'm in." Fortunately, most of us are not behind bars. But how many of us have walled off our hearts in an effort to make ourselves less vulnerable? If childhood hurts didn't shut us down, the pressure to succeed by society's definitions may have. It doesn't happen overnight, but the accumulation of trade-offs and compromises can slowly numb us to our heart's instincts.

While I was suffering from the uncertainty of my illness, I rarely wept. I felt that if I started to come apart, I might not be able to pull myself together again. Gradually, as the walls to my heart came down, I discovered that my willingness to feel my lows gave me access to more of me. Not just my creativity and love, but my faith in the movement of life itself. Now I can be strong *and* soft. I have more of myself to share, and I feel more profoundly connected. Wholeness is in our nature, and when we allow and acknowledge our feelings, we claim more of who we really are.

Grief to Gladness

Judith Orloff, MD, author of *Emotional Freedom*, writes that every emotion is born of either fear or love. That means hatred, frustration, disappointment, regret, shame, insecurity, loneliness, anxiety, worry, depression, jealousy, envy, and anger are born of *fear*, and reverence, happiness, courage, hope, wonder, self-esteem, patience, compassion, generosity, gratitude, enthusiasm, and elation are born of *love*.

Bliss is our natural state and a magnet for everything good. When we feel good for no reason, it confirms we're navigating on course. By trusting our instincts to do more of what feels like a "yes!" and thinking thoughts that uplift us, we produce joyful feelings that attract more of the same. That doesn't mean you should feel ashamed if you feel lonely, jealous, or afraid. It's a healthy sign if you can feel a wide range of feelings, and all emotions guide us. Emotions and feelings are waves of energy passing through, inviting us to transform!

Authentic emotions run the gamut from grief to gladness. We recognize that an emotion is authentic because of its fluid nature. Like clouds scudding across the sky, feelings move and morph as we acknowledge their presence. It's only when we're stuck in a feeling that we can't seem to shake that we need to excavate. At these times, we are likely telling ourselves a story about the situation or feeling, and probably haven't yet felt the depth of the authentic emotion that resides below.

Comedian Swami Beyondananda teaches us the purpose of negativity, saying, "Life is like photography—you use the negative to develop!" Negative emotions—those born of fear—are not bad; they are nature's way of asking us to wake up to our deeper intelligence.

The heart is wise. It is where we exclude nothing. When we're in our heart, we create unity and inclusiveness for everyone and everything. It is there that we find the patience and compassion to accept our own imperfections, as well as the faith and the courage to change. A friend reminds me, "The road will not get any less bumpy, so lean back and enjoy the ride in the limousine of your heart."

Looking Ahead

In the rest of this chapter you will access the power of your emotional intelligence and unlock the love and joy that abide in your heart.

By waking the wisdom of your heart you will:

- Be more aware of what you are feeling when you are feeling it.
- Free yourself from emotional upsets that cause you to spiral down.
- Learn to cultivate feelings of happiness, love, joy, and gratitude.
- Listen to your feelings as clues nudging you toward what brings you alive.

Stories

So many of our difficult feelings have their roots in childhood, as the stories here illustrate. We may try to think our way out of painful feelings, but there is a more effective way. By enlisting the patient compassion of our hearts, we not only mend the original wound, we discover its gift. The French word for wound or hurt is *blessure*. Wounds are blessings because they shatter the armor of our personality so that we may live more nakedly from our hearts.

Caitlan's Story: Toughing It Out

Twelve-year-old Caitlan was unpacking her schoolbag when her younger brother, Kevin, burst through the front door, hair and clothes rumpled, tears streaming down his face. He fled to the kitchen, only to run smack into their dad, home unexpectedly early from work. "What happened to you?" their father bellowed.

Red in the face, Kevin muttered, "I was jumped by bullies."

The blow came hard and fast to Kevin's soft center. Caitlan could feel her brother's pain as he cried out and folded over, coughing. His father yelled at him, "We're no cowards! Get back out there and stick up for yourself!"

Caitlan's father was teaching his son a lesson in the only way he knew how. He understood his kids would need tough skins to survive growing up in their small town outside of Cork, Ireland, where feelings weren't coddled or even acknowledged.

Many of us receive messages as children that we carry into adulthood. For Caitlan, the message was to hang tough and never show her fear or softer feelings. Inside, she felt she wasn't good enough, but this only sharpened her determination to succeed. She won a coveted spot at a prestigious private school, was the first in her family to go to university, and later moved to the United States to work her way up in the ranks of a global pharmaceutical company.

With a prestigious title, reporting directly to the CEO, Caitlan enjoyed the power and visibility afforded by her position. But when a merger and subsequent layoffs created a highly political environment, Caitlan lost her VP title and was assigned a new boss.

Caitlan felt compelled to do whatever it took to hang on to her influence. Because she associated fear with weakness, she overcompensated by making preemptive strikes and subtle threats against real or imagined adversaries. Her ingrained reactive pattern of sticking up for herself when under pressure kept her fixated on keeping what she had, instead of opening her hands to what the universe was offering. She put in long hours, engaging in what seemed like a work-off competition with other employees to see who would be the last one to leave at night. Her days were tense and her nights sleepless. Numb to her true feelings and fueled by fear, Caitlan was fighting a war she could never win.

One aspect of her job did light her up, however. She was part of a leadership program for selected executives. Once a month she interacted with inspired entrepreneurs, "social capitalists" who had transcended difficult life experiences to create companies that were making a difference. She identified with these hardscrabble achievers and wanted to be more like them.

One weekend, thumbing through an old photo album, Caitlan was struck by her photo from an earlier time—head thrown back, laughing, light in her eyes. Sadly she wondered, "Where has that woman gone?"

Fear short-circuits our connection to our true self—especially when we don't acknowledge that we're feeling it. However, as we recognize what fear feels like in our bodies, thoughts, and feelings, we can unplug from it. When fearful, we lose touch with our peace and the core truth of our existence—that we are loved.

It was essential for Caitlan to see that the universe was trying to show her a new way forward. I asked Caitlan if she could tell the difference between her fear mode and her real self. She replied, "When my fear voice is in control, I stop breathing, I sound shrill and intense. But when I'm listening to my knowing voice, I feel strong and clear. I'm on both feet, alive. I breathe deep, hold my shoulders back, and feel taller." Caitlan could now distinguish between the mind's fears and her heart's knowing.

The spiral path teaches us that what pained us in childhood often sculpts our unique gift for the world. Often the fiery pain from our unmet needs forges the capacity to give the very thing we long for. Our "flaw" becomes our gift. Caitlan had been ashamed of her feelings. But she now realized that what she perceived as her weakness was her ability to feel deeply and passionately about what needed to change.

Caitlan didn't have to try to stop defending her ego's agenda; it just lost its allure as she became more like the social entrepreneurs she so admired. Soon after, she was offered a position with a socially conscious start-up and went on to lead an organization that was making a powerful difference in the world. More importantly, Caitlan's dry sense of humor and infectious laugh are now always part of her day.

> As your fears begin to leave you, your interest and care in others will increase. Your life will begin to fill with the meaning and purpose and joy that you were born to experience—that you were born to create.
>
> —Gary Zukav

Exercises

Sadness and fear, uplift and joy, come and go in every life—sometimes all in the same day! In the exercises here, you will learn ways to care for your changing feelings and nurture your own tender places within.

What Am I Feeling?

We don't plan to feel fearful, stressed out, angry, or sad. In fact, when uncomfortable feelings bubble up, we may judge ourselves and try to shut them down. But feelings can be catalysts for our growth and aliveness.

The word *emotion* comes from the Latin for "to move." We might feel teary in the morning, angry by afternoon, and joyful by evening. To assist emotions in flowing instead of taking up residence in our bodies, hearts, and psyches, we must first receive them, just as we did with thoughts when we learned to harness the Co-Creative Power of Mind. By increasing our awareness of what we are feeling, we build our capacity to accept our feelings and benefit from the valuable information they offer. By witnessing (not being overtaken by) any waves of emotion passing through, we become more resilient.

Think of a time you felt a "pinch" (an emotion that made you contract inside). Identify at least three adjectives that best describe how you felt at the time, both physically and emotionally. Examples: guilty, sad, ashamed.

Now, think of a time when you felt an "uplift" (an emotion that made you feel expansive). Select at least three adjectives that best describe your experience. Examples: energized, calm, loved.

The next time you experience a "pinch" or "uplift," notice if, by identifying the actual body sensations and emotional truth of your feeling, you are freed to experience a fuller range of emotion.

It is the place of feelings that binds us or frees us.
—Jack Kornfield

Extinguish the Fire

Emotional upsets can occur when we feel slighted or when things don't go the way we expected. Pointing fingers only throws fuel on the fire. If you want to put out the fire, turn your finger to point back at yourself, not to condemn but to take responsibility for your experience.

The next time you feel a "pinch," compassionately ask yourself the following questions and sense how your upset loses its charge:

1. What am I *really* upset about?
2. What was my part in this upset?
3. Am I committed to being peaceful or being right?
4. Can I let my heart forgive any actions or inactions on my own part or the part of others?

Everything that irritates us about others can lead us to an understanding of ourselves.

—Carl Jung

Befriend Fear

Think of FEAR as an acronym for False Evidence Appearing Real. As Caitlan discovered when she acknowledged her "fear voice," by facing our fears we can dispel them.

1. What are you afraid of? Identify at least five fears. Examples: I will end up old and alone, I will be stuck in a job I hate forever, I will never get out of debt.

Often it's our younger self who carries our biggest fears. She is the part of us that needs protection and care. Once you've listed your fears, imagine lifting your younger self up and placing her on your lap. Now connect with the grown up, wise, resourceful part of you. From that place, assure your inner "little girl" that you will be there for her no matter what happens. Remind her that she can rely on you, a strong and capable woman who can deal effectively with whatever comes.

If your "little girl" still feels fearful, ask her the following question.

2. What do you need in order to feel safe? Listen carefully to what she has to say and write down her responses.

3. Make an effort to create one of those conditions today. Examples: In order to feel safe, my "little girl" needs me: to take better care of myself, to make time to join the softball team, to take charge of my accounts. Take one concrete action, no matter how small. Notice whether it makes you feel more peaceful inside.

I need to take an emotional breath, step back and remind myself who's actually in charge of my life.

—Judith Knowlton

Highlights

- Our hearts can comprehend meaning without words.
- When we're in touch with our heart's knowing, we get answers to our questions.
- Our ability to process uncomfortable feelings helps us feel more alive.
- Caitlan shows us how our "flaw" can become our gift.
- You've learned a three-step process for diffusing fear.
- You can increase emotional awareness by tuning in to your body's signals.

CHAPTER 6

Architect a Juicy Life with Words of Plenty

The Co-Creative Power of Speech

The words you speak become the house you live in.
—Attributed to Hafiz

When I was little, my Irish uncle used to call me "banana mouth" because I would usually say whatever was on my mind. His nickname for me was his way of playfully reminding me that I fit right in with the loquacious side of my family.

Like many girls in adolescence, at some point I realized that good girls didn't speak their minds. I didn't want to be perceived as being too loud, too bossy, or too much. Good girls kept quiet, never talked back, and always let others take the lead. I remember attempting to adopt that whole philosophy. I tried to tamp down my natural ability to speak the truth in order to fit in and be liked.

But it didn't last long. My need to speak directly and forthrightly won out. As a coach I found it incredibly satisfying to support women in finding words for what they needed to say, in ways that could be received. In helping them find their voices, I cultivated more of my own.

The Co-Creative Power of Speech is our capacity to use words to positively evolve a situation or bring something new into being. It is the act of being genuine and intentional about what we choose to vocalize. Because you've already activated your Co-Creative Powers of Energy, Mind, and Feelings, your ability to speak in ways that support your own and others' upliftment will come naturally. Now you are perfectly poised to take advantage of the wonderment of words.

"In the beginning was the Word," we read in the Gospel of John, and sacred texts in many traditions proclaim that *the word* is our foundational reality. Many indigenous peoples' origin stories hold that in the beginning was the *sound*. In the Genesis account of creation, God speaks the world into being: "God said, Let there be light; and there was light." In biblical Hebrew, the word *davar* literally means both "word" and "thing."

Consciousness, or mind, is the original raw material with which we co-create, and words are an extension of consciousness. We comprehend reality by noting and distinguishing something from its background, giving it a name, and calling it by a word. Walking barefoot on a beach we feel the soft, loose grains and call it "sand." We look to the sky and think of the floating white fluffy things as "clouds." This process of naming things is not only how we bring things into focus, it is how we co-create reality.

Singling out things from their surroundings and labeling them happens so automatically that we're normally not aware of it, and we typically move through our days without using words as the inventive tools that they are. But we can learn to use our speech intentionally to consciously shape our reality. In doing so, we begin to align the power of words with our desire to make the world a better place. We literally talk our way into a more inspired future.

Language Is an Action

Just as a pebble creates ripples in the pond where it is tossed, words have powerful reverberations. All it takes is one cruel appraisal from someone we trust and our wings are clipped, our psyche marked for years. On the other hand, heartfelt praise or encouraging words from an admired ally can fuel us for a lifetime. Bruce Lipton, a cellular biologist, points to the impact of thoughts and words in his research in cell physiology. His findings reveal that virtually every one of our cellular functions is impacted by the electromagnetic fields—the invisible energy forces—produced by our thoughts and words. Knowing this, it's important to be conscious of how we are composing our life scripts with our words.

But often, instead of choosing our words mindfully, out of habit we speak haphazardly, reporting or describing our experience from our ever-changing perspective. We rarely take into account the fact that the way we characterize things is self-fulfilling. For instance, it matters how I answer the question, "How are you?" If I launch into a tirade about how my alarm clock didn't go off, how there was an accident on the way to work, and how my nosy coworker made a comment when I walked in late, does this inspire me to reach my potential? Or have I spiraled myself down?

Try this for yourself right now. Say these words aloud and notice the repercussions on your body and soul.

I can't do it. Life is hopeless.

Now try...

I am powerful! Life is full of possibilities!

Did you notice the heaviness in your body when you spoke of hopelessness? Did you experience a sense of uplift when you declared your power and the fullness of life's potential?

Language can awaken or poison possibilities. How might we speak differently if we remembered that every word we utter lays down the blueprint for what's next?

Speaking from the Heart

What Buddhists call right speech comes naturally when we're connected with our Co-Creative Powers of Energy, Mind, and Feelings. These powerful portals to presence connect us to our inner knowing and awareness. From this expansive state, our minds, hearts, and lips agree. For example, if our energy is flowing and our heart and mind are aligned, our words easily reach others. And, as with all your other Co-Creative Powers, shifting your consciousness in one creates a chain effect and the rest align. No matter what my thoughts are doing, if I can make the conscious effort to speak from a place of generosity and kindness, my energy, mind, feelings, and actions will soon follow.

When we're disconnected from our other Co-Creative Powers, however, it's much harder to speak intentionally or to remember that our words are vehicles for transformation. Think of the last time you felt inhibited about speaking your truth. You might have had a sense of what you wanted to say, but because it wasn't perfectly formed, you held back. Perhaps you felt you had to talk your way out of a difficult situation. Maybe your face flushed or you felt hot in your solar plexus. In those moments, we may find ourselves withholding or twisting the truth in an attempt to protect ourselves, control things, change the way people react to us, or get what we want. We might speak disingenuously to avoid causing conflict, hurting people's feelings, or appearing foolish. Gossiping is another form of inauthentic communication. It might make us feel momentarily superior to others or bonded with our confidante, but it also sacrifices our integrity.

When we're fearful, we lose touch with our innate wisdom and our communication gets tainted. Speaking courageously from the heart immediately anchors us in our true essence and power. This doesn't mean you'll be baldly frank, saying whatever comes to mind no matter how brutal. Rather, it means being able to say, "I disagree even if the rest of you agree." It is your capacity to speak up in a meeting even if you aren't sure that you know the right answer.

Later in the book I will show you ways to find your authentic voice: to use your words to make difficult requests, establish boundaries, and purge negativity all while staying related and connected to others.

As you become more skillful with your Co-Creative Power of Speech, you will discover how to recast your words to redesign your life. Speech is an extraordinary power: it can inspire nations, heal broken hearts, make love, denounce injustice, or calm a crying child. And it can help you to define and create an extraordinary existence. As you delve deeper into this vital capacity, you will learn to do as the late Buddhist poet, writer, and activist Thich Nhat Hanh did: "I vow to learn to speak truthfully, with words that inspire self-confidence, joy, and hope."

Speech Checkup

> Reflect upon each of these questions, and answer them on the continuum of "mostly," "sometimes," "rarely," or "never."
>
> Are you intentional with your words?
> Do you speak from your heart?
> Are your communications honest?
> Do your words inspire and uplift others?

Find a quiet space where you won't be overheard and speak a truth out loud. See how your energy, feelings, and thoughts shift as your words fill the space around you.

Sufficiency Speaking

Three stonecutters in the fourteenth century are working in the noonday sun. A curious passerby asks the first stonecutter what he is doing, to which he replies, "A foot by a foot, by three-fourths of a foot, over and over I cut this stone into blocks until the day I die."

Walking farther along, the man comes upon a second stonecutter, who is also cutting stone into blocks. The man asks the stonecutter what he is doing. The stonecutter explains, "I am earning a living so that my beloved family has food to grow strong, clothes to stay warm, and a home filled with love."

As the man approaches the third stonecutter, he is greeted with a radiant smile. The stonecutter proclaims, "Behold this sacred cathedral that I have the privilege of helping to build! It will stand as a holy lighthouse for thousands of years!"

In every instance, we can choose words that give us hope and inspire us, or words that keep us trapped in a little life. We can give voice to stories that connect and make us feel part of the whole, or stories that make us feel separate and alone. We can speak automatically and unconsciously, or we can connect with our hearts and speak our truth.

Before we can speak consciously we must get good at listening, both to others and to ourselves. With a little mindfulness, we can catch any circulating "lack stories" and steer our minds toward thoughts of gratitude and plenty. It was once said that the longest journey we must take is the eighteen inches from our head to our heart. Dropping down into the goodwill of our hearts, we'll more likely choose words that enliven and empower and engage us in conversations centered on possibility rather than on what's missing. I call this Sufficiency Speaking.

When Stacie, a participant in my Spiral Up! series, took on the class's forty-eight-hour Sufficiency Speaking challenge, she was eager to start her "fast" from negativity. The following day she got her chance as she was preparing for an upcoming marathon with a ten-mile run. Stacie mentally practiced her Sufficiency Speaking throughout the run and shared the results. "Instead of getting hijacked by worries, I kept telling myself I'm strong and well prepared to run these ten miles. Mile by mile I focused on my strong legs, thankful for my good health. I was very aware of my surroundings and the wonderful smells along the trail—the fresh air, many types of trees and shrubbery. Thinking in sufficiency made the ten-mile trek so much easier than other long runs."

Sufficiency Speaking can be challenging because we live in a not-enough culture. The idea of scarcity is widely accepted (limited opportunities, love, joy, friends, recognition). How often has your first thought of the morning been, "I didn't get enough sleep"? It's human to notice what's missing or not enough. In fact, because shared hardships are often the stuff that forges friendships, we are inclined to think sharing mutual inadequacies or comparing war stories about everything from in-laws to physical ailments is the only way to build bonds. But if these bonds are based on our wounds and failings, the built-in reward system propagates more of the same.

Mainstream media thrive on bad news and sensationalize the negative. Advertising rivets our attention on what we're missing so that we feel compelled to go buy it, and news fixates on drama that is horrific, gloomy, or threatening. It's so insidious that it saturates our consciousness and infiltrates our conversations: the downturn, the unfair boss, our diminishing 401(k), our wrinkles. Worse still, this constant stream of fear-based "deficit" communication steals our energy and attention from the real challenges we face. We spiral down anytime we blame, complain, or speak disparagingly about anyone, including ourselves. It's critical to be intentional about the message you want to convey.

How do you want to impact people? Are you communicating to build bridges or to manipulate or control? Will what you say perpetuate fear or leave others in better shape than you found them? To Spiral Up! we must shift ourselves from the ubiquitous party line of scarcity—"something's wrong"—to a sense of fullness and generosity that is anchored in our connection with everything else. From this vantage point of sufficiency we feel an impulse to share and contribute, and we naturally employ the power of words to forward possibilities.

In other words, we can choose to change the story. Conscious "Sufficiency Speaking" is life changing—and can be life saving.

Creating a New Reality with Words

Visionary activist Caroline Casey tells the story of her friend, a UN relief worker, who was kidnapped with colleagues in a war zone right after they had found friends slain by the side of the road. As they rode along in the back of their captors' van with guns to their heads, they started to lose hope. When they arrived at the camp, the UN worker said to his colleagues, "We've got to change the story. We're not being kidnapped, we're being helped." They began to thank their kidnappers for keeping them safe in such a complex environment. The kidnappers were puzzled. But later that night, as they were being locked up, the leader said to them: "Don't worry. We're putting a guard outside so you'll be safe." Three days later, they let them go.

Lera Boroditsky, associate professor of cognitive science at the University of California, San Diego, discovered that when we speak differently, we think differently. Collecting data from China, Greece, Chile, Indonesia, Russia, and Aboriginal Australia, her research revealed that language and thought are inextricably related. As she puts it, "Even flukes of grammar can profoundly affect how we see the world." In an age when language is often reduced to talking points, sound bites, and advertising slogans, it takes initiative to speak in ways that are authentic and positively impactful to ourselves and those who hear us.

That doesn't mean we should never voice concerns, worries, or objections. When we feel stuck, women instinctively know that to get our energy moving again, it often helps to talk about it. In *The Artist's Way*, Julia Cameron prescribes "morning pages," a powerful exercise that involves writing three pages, stream of consciousness, first thing every morning as a way to clear out mental and emotional impediments to becoming your most creative self. We can also "outflow" to a committed listener. This is someone who won't add to our "story" by jumping in with her own bad experience or by commiserating about how awful ours is, but who will support us in our stated intention to let go and move beyond what's troubling us.

Self-awareness—noticing what we're thinking and how we're interacting with the world—is a powerful first step. To truly transform through the Co-Creative Power of Speech we must first become aware of our impulse to react, feel the tension between our habitual verbal response and who we'd like to be, and make a different choice.

Looking Ahead

As you engage the Co-Creative Power of Speech in this chapter, you will learn how to speak in ways that spread goodness and truth, as well as express your full self, in the world.

By speaking from sufficiency you will learn to:

- Be intentional with the messages you convey
- Shift conversations from negative to positive
- Create a positive reality with your words
- Become *fluent* in acknowledgment and appreciation

Do not be critics, you people, I beg you. I was a critic and I wish I could take it all back because it came from a smelly and ignorant place in me and spoke with a voice that was all rage and envy.

—Dave Eggers

Stories

Our words shape our world, whether we're aware of it or not. The following stories offer examples of how to become more skillful in speaking, not in a habitual, descriptive way—where we just create what we already have—but in an authentic, inventive way, where we bring more of our true self forward and consciously call the future we want into being.

Anna's Story: From Woundedness to Possibility

Anna had just separated from her husband of twenty-five years. She thought a temporary separation might catalyze a change that would eventually bring them closer. Much to her surprise, her husband started dating and within a few weeks was intimately involved with another woman. The sudden and irrevocable loss of her relationship seemed overwhelming. What made it more difficult was the close proximity in which they lived. She worried that she might bump into the "happy couple" in their small town. Almost more painful were her actual run-ins with neighbors or acquaintances who would sympathetically inquire, "How *are* you?"

The produce section of your local grocery store is not usually the best place to broach the unfinished business of the heart. Yet Anna's feelings of abandonment and rejection were so close to the surface that when others expressed curiosity, she replied with the first thing that came to mind, which was often some expression of her difficulty and pain. Each time she relived her story she spun into a downward spiral of anger and resentment. Worse yet, her painful disclosures often evoked others' stories of heartbreak and betrayal, stirring her up in ways that took days to recover from.

It might feel "authentic" in the moment to go on about what's wrong. But to what end? Each time Anna told the story of her separation, she recycled old feelings and inflamed inner wounds. As many of us experience when we're hurting, Anna found herself caught up in reciting her problems when she really wanted to clear them away.

We have a choice about how we talk about the challenges in our lives. When we speak from sufficiency, we move from fear to aspiration and eventually to inspiration. We communicate with others in ways that allow us to see beyond our woundedness to the potential and possibility in every situation. Learning to speak from a place of sufficiency doesn't mean that we twist the truth—just turn it to reflect the light. The question became: How could Anna be truthful while taking care of herself?

Working together, Anna and I composed a response that allowed her to remain honest while also attending to her higher intentions. She needed a way of replying to people's concerns that left her feeling positive and clear.

When people asked, "How *are* you?" Anna learned to say, "I'm all right. I've made some big changes that needed to be made for quite awhile. Of course, there are growing pains, yet at the same time I'm optimistic about what's next. In fact, I'm exploring some new avenues I'm really excited about." With this last statement, Anna steered the conversation from deficiency to sufficiency. And in the process, gained the enthusiastic support of others in creating her new life.

Randy's Story: Accentuate the Positive

The idea that appreciation brings out the best in people became undeniably obvious to me at a Christmas party years ago. I was there with Charles, a former boyfriend whom I had known since high school. Charles, who had silky amber skin, salt-and-pepper hair, and refined but masculine features, was somewhat reserved, a dark and silent type that many girls considered "hot" in high school. However, over the last thirty years Charles had gained an equal number of pounds. Knowing how dashing he could be, I somehow felt it was my duty to point out ways he might begin to get into better shape. If he went for seconds or ate a big piece of cake, I would make a disapproving face. I constantly bugged him to join a health club and talked about the virtues of building core muscles in Pilates. There were times when I was downright thoughtless, almost mean. Until "game night" at Randy's Christmas party.

Randy, a brilliant coach, could inspire a turtle to win a race. As we played Scene-It, a movie trivia game, each time Charles got anything close to right, she would cheer him on in a heartfelt way. "Charles, that was great! How did you know that? I'm so glad we're on the same team." A bit socially awkward, Charles would typically go silent rather than guess wrong and risk embarrassment. But as the game heated up, Charles loosened up. Suddenly he was flinging answers out of nowhere and accurately naming actors in movies I was sure he hadn't even seen! As Randy egged him on, this soft-spoken guy became the life of the party. My mouth dropped open as he aced the final answers and raised his arms in victory to the cheers of his team. In the warmth of Randy's appreciation and encouragement, Charles was transformed.

I knew that goading people to change often had the reverse effect, and in this case it left me feeling bad about myself too. Randy showed me that appreciation transforms not only the recipient, but also—even more so—the person who generates the acknowledgment. She explained, "When you speak from the heart, you feel your love and deep appreciation of the other; nothing else can be present in that moment." With Randy's modeling, I learned to coach my clients to become fluent in acknowledging people for ordinary acts—for showing up, for smiling, for being themselves—instead of waiting to "reward" people for exceptional deeds. This is a key skill that distinguishes extraordinary leaders and engaged workplaces, enlightened parents and thriving families, and loving partners and long-term relationships.

When one intends to move or speak, one should first examine one's own mind and then act appropriately with composure.

—Shantideva

One Teacher's Story—Life-Changing Words

Spiritual teacher Jack Kornfield shared the following story at a Monday night sitting at Spirit Rock Meditation Center.

A math teacher with a boisterous and disorderly class tested the power of appreciation a few days before summer break. Her class had a few troublemakers in it, but this day everyone seemed out of control; no one was paying attention. She shut her lesson plan book and announced, "We're not going to do math today."

She then proceeded to write the names of each student on the blackboard and asked everyone to list one or two good things about each of his classmates. She collected the lists, and at the end of the school year she returned a personalized list to the students with all the appreciative things their classmates had written about them.

Three years later she got a call from the mother of one of her students. He'd been killed serving in the First Gulf War in Kuwait. "It's important that you come to the funeral," she told the teacher. "He loved you."

Arriving at the funeral, the teacher was pulled aside by the boy's mother. "They sent back what my son carried with him in the desert. I thought you should see this." Yellowed, torn, and folded many times over, it was the paper containing his classmates' words of praise. As the mother spoke softly to the small congregation, she described her son with the words that had touched him so deeply. Unexpectedly, a woman from the back row raised her hand and said, "I carry mine too!" Another former classmate shared that he had his with him, and that they were read at his wedding.

This math teacher had planted the seeds of enduring beauty during that one class. And that day, in that church, despite all the tears, they were still blooming.

Exercises

We hold the keys to great power in our expression of the spoken word. But we're just learning how to use our powers, and evolving ourselves takes work—it doesn't happen by itself. The following exercises will help you hear what you're really saying and start to shift your words in the direction of a higher truth.

> **Mind your speech a little lest you should mar your fortunes.**
>
> **—William Shakespeare**

Sufficiency Speaking in Action

Do you tend to speak from sufficiency or from lack? Ask yourself the following questions and note the answer that most often applies.

Do you routinely speak harshly of others or of circumstances?
Do you verbally criticize or negatively compare yourself?
Do you play down your positive qualities by being self-effacing?

If you answered yes to any of the questions above, don't get down on yourself—that's exactly what we're trying to avoid. Knowing your "weak" spots will help you speak from sufficiency in the future.

Which areas of your life do you speak about from deficiency or lack? Identify at least three areas. Examples: my work life, my body, my finances.

For the areas you consider to be your weak spots, list three things that you can appreciate and then say them out loud. Write your appreciations in the first person and in complete sentences. If your work life is an area where you speak from lack, you might discover: "I am grateful for the autonomy my job gives me." In your relationship with your body, it might be: "I like the way my body moves when I dance."

By listing your appreciations and then speaking them aloud, you'll begin to activate the Co-Creative Power of Speech to help you rise in confidence and self-assurance.

You achieve much once you stop telling yourself you can't do things.

—**Elizabeth Kadetsky**

Conscious Venting

When our emotions run hot we women need to find ways to let it all out. Bottling it up creates combustion that will eventually find an outlet, often at the most inappropriate moment. Our need for a sympathetic ear is perfectly legit!

Find a friend for mutual and conscious venting. Someone you can call and say, "I need to outflow for two minutes." As your committed listener, she or he will support you in calming and releasing your energy, not throwing more logs on the fire by adding to your "story."

"Up Until Now..."

Words are symbols that point to something. Our words aim our attention and can either lift us up or knock us down. It takes mindfulness and intention to speak from sufficiency, which causes an upward gravitational pull. The benefits are well worth the effort.

Try the following technique, until it feels natural and easy. If you tend to speak about something you consider a "fault," in ways that minimize your capabilities, try prefacing your "flaw" with "Up until now..." Examples:

Instead of "I don't have enough willpower to lose weight," say: "Up until now, I haven't been motivated enough to be more fit and healthy."
Instead of "I never get chosen for a promotion," say: "Up until now, I haven't been chosen for a promotion."
Instead of "I'll never meet my soul mate," say: "Up until now, I haven't met my soul mate."

Think of one of your most common complaints or criticisms, then shift it by completing this sentence: "Up until now _____."

Highlights

- We can use our words to consciously shape our reality.
- Language is an action because it is a creative force that has a ripple effect.
- Speaking from sufficiency versus deficiency allows for greater possibilities.
- Speaking courageously from the heart immediately anchors us in our true essence.
- Like Randy, we empower others (and ourselves) through appreciation, not criticism.
- We can speak of difficult situations in ways that are both honest and caring.

CHAPTER 7

Be True to Your Soul's Intent

The Co-Creative Power of Action

When sleeping women wake, mountains move.
—Chinese proverb

By now you probably understand why I believe so passionately in the five Co-Creative Powers. But writing a book about them was another matter—I had never taken a writing class, I didn't even know anyone who had actually written a book. I didn't know how to do it but I knew deep down that it was mine to do. Then, over a decade ago, I offered to give a talk to a group of clients. I had only the bare bones of the Spiral Up! concept at the time. In fact, I was a little shocked at myself for committing to the talk because I wasn't at all sure what I would say.

Between the day I agreed to speak and the day I delivered the first Spiral Up! speech, all the key ideas and structure of the book came to me. Of course, it took some years to actually flesh it out. But that divine "download" would not have happened had I not reached for something bigger by committing to that talk.

This has been my secret to success—listening to what my soul desires and saying yes (even if I am trembling while giving the speech, signing the lease, or committing to the project). When I say yes to something that both excites and scares me I am no longer just living, life is living me!

Congratulate yourself! You have arrived at the Co-Creative Power of Action on the wings of all the transformational work you've done so far in your Spiral Up! journey. You now have liftoff!

We are here on Earth to self-ACTualize: to fulfill our potential and to become the most authentic expression of our highest selves. As you work through this first section of the book, you are beginning to move beyond your small, biographical self into your most wondrous potential. You may be beginning to see how your inner gifts sync up with the unmet needs in the world. New ways and means to live your purpose will emerge as you progress through the chapters ahead.

In order to create a glorious "alivelihood," inspired action must be a part of your journey. To self-ACTualize, you must ACT—and not in a careless or hollow way, but on behalf of the woman you were born to be.

Action is the final Co-Creative Power because it is the natural by-product of the internal shift that takes place within you through working with your energy, mind, feelings, and speech. Action is where you get to walk your talk and be the change! It is the bridge between dreams and reality. It is where you show up and step out in alignment with your deepest integrity and soul's purpose. This is where miracles can occur—sometimes glitzy, *bling*-big miracles, sometimes small and tender ones. But the miracles are always personal, meaningful, and exciting.

A wise philosopher once said, "By far the best proof is experience." Or, as I like to say, by *doing* we come to *know* it in our bones. Our actions can and do change our physiology and brain chemistry. Can you remember the first time you drove a car, sent an e-mail, or kissed a lover? When we experience something for the first time, new knowledge is stored in our body's cellular memory and we are forever changed. We occupy a bigger space; we claim more ground.

Too Busy for Our Own Good

Yet not all actions lead us where our souls want to go. Inspired action can prove elusive as we juggle too many tasks, race to meet self-imposed and external deadlines, and remain senselessly busy. We often work so hard to make money and maintain our lifestyles that we feel too drained to respond to our deeper calling. Many of us find it hard to believe that working at what we love is economically feasible. Meanwhile, pedal to the metal, we rush into action, often bypassing the road signs that point to our true destination. Pure masculine drive without feminine receptivity is like an unguided missile.

But when we work with the universal energy of the spiral, our feminine receptivity informs our direction. We become aware of what we want by encountering what we don't want. With self-awareness, we discover who we are by realizing who we are not. We recognize that the very challenge that we face right now is shaping us into our greater self. Our feminine receptivity allows us to be transformed by life's lessons, and our masculine self enables us to act from this new place. In tune with our inner guidance, we know what is ours to do. Even in the face of fear, we are empowered to act with integrity and heart. Stewarded by the upward impulse of the spiral, we no longer depend on sheer will and effort.

Peter Senge, scientist and director at the MIT Sloan School of Management, points out that "many scientists and inventors, like artists and entrepreneurs, live in a paradoxical state of great confidence and profound humility—knowing that their choices and actions really matter and feeling guided by forces beyond their making. Their work is to 'release the hand from the marble that holds it prisoner,' as Michelangelo put it." When we're in sync with the spiral, while we know our actions are vital to our accomplishments, we also come to understand that our hand wants to be released. We sense our greater selves coming through.

A Sense of Grace

It's such a relief to know that it's not all up to us! As we partner with the magnificent life force that flows through the spiral, we are acted upon rather than acting alone. We trust the inherent order and timing of things. We align with the subtle unfolding of what wants to emerge, and our actions become imbued with a sense of grace and synchronicity. It's like when we get "lost" down some side street, only to discover an obscure store specializing in the exact thing we had given up finding, or when we come across a line in a book that answers a burning question we didn't even know we had.

This isn't a passive attitude but a vehement "yes" to our inner calling. You act because you feel in your heart—in your gut—this is who I'm supposed to be, this is where I'm supposed to go, this is what I'm supposed to do and say and this is the person to whom I should say it. When we're in touch with these instincts, we feel a greater sense of clarity and agency. We know in our hearts what fulfillment looks like, and we're willing to take bold action on behalf of it.

It's triumphant to wake up to life. I feel a tremendous sense of liberation. You want to be able to use both your intuitive side and your go-get-'em side!

—Meg Ryan

Inspired action happens naturally when we pay attention to the moments when we feel most alive and engaged. They whet our appetites for more opportunities that resonate with our hearts, and even though they might feel outside our comfort zone, we go for it! We devote time, energy, and attention to what lights us up. By being open to our divine ideas and inner cues, as well as the clues from our environment, we continually tack in the direction of our soul's promise, finding and expressing more and more of our unique gifts.

As you explore the Co-Creative Power of Action, you'll be empowered to take little risks outside your comfort zone and move into your "zone of possibility." Reading through the stories and engaging with the exercises and practices, you'll see how to navigate through obstacles that have stopped you in the past. No matter where you work or what you're doing, you'll become inspired to find creative ways to use your unique set of gifts and strengths.

You'll be reminded that even one small step in the direction of what lights you up can change the course of your journey and lead you to fulfillment.

This is inspired action.

Actions Checkup

Reflect upon each of these questions, and answer them on the continuum of "mostly," "sometimes," "rarely," or "never."

Are you walking your talk?
Are you aware of what actions bring you alive?
Are your actions in service of your calling?
Do you act outside your comfort zone?

Toward an Inspired Life

We're here on earth to self-ACTualize, to do the work of our soul, our highest self. There is nothing more important than undertaking life's grand adventure of discovering our potential and using it to make a difference in the world.

The trouble is, most of us are so busy getting our basic needs met that our soul's purpose tends to take a back seat.

We can also get stuck at our own comfort level. We gain a certain degree of regard or material success and we begin to rest on our laurels and imitate ourselves. We may feel like we're creating and evolving, but we're actually *re*creating and *re*volving, doing the same things over and over again. Yet the seeds of our greater self are always within us.

In order to self-ACTualize, we have to move beyond our ego motivations and begin to embody our full potential. Your spirit or soul is the impetus in you to want to be better, do better, and make the world a better place. It can easily be confused with the voice of the ego that just wants more things, accomplishments, or experiences in order to feel enough. We know that we're evolving beyond ego motivation when simply chalking up "more" is no longer enough.

It's important to identify what is motivating our actions. Inspired action is acting on behalf of what brings you alive. Ask yourself, "What are my actions on behalf of? How true am I being to my soul's intent?" We're all giving our lives to something, devoting our lives to something, essentially "worshipping" something; it's just a question of what.

Making Space for Truth

If most of our actions are on behalf of money or things, when our soul calls, no one answers. That's when addictions flare. Jungian analyst and author Marion Woodman said that we are basically chalices, and that our chalices can be filled with busyness, alcohol, drugs, shopping, or perfectionism, or filled with spirit: our higher self. We are not bottomless cups to be filled again and again only to remain empty. We are fulfilled through the giving of our gifts, through the living of our values—our soul's work.

If you've been hearing the call of your soul but you haven't picked up the phone, you may start to feel out of sorts, even antsy; you may eat too much, watch too much TV, and, if your perfectionism kicks in, fall prey to self-judgment and self-criticism. But it's no accident that there's an "ow" in the word *grow*. Chaos and disruption are part of the transformational process. Conflict is just the universe egging you on to leave the small, the old, the confining for something more life-giving, expansive, and effervescent. If you're standing at that crossroads right now, you have a choice to get bitter or better, to stay stuck and be a victim or take inspired actions that will move you forward on your heroine's journey.

There's truth in the statement "When mama's happy, everybody's happy." You may have to get a little selfish at first. You'll need to stop breaking your promises to yourself and put your needs at the top of the list. If you're down-hearted, you'll start by religiously providing yourself with whatever you need to feel whole again. It may take time. Sometimes our greatest acts involve doing nothing but sitting and waiting until we know what to do next. It may take lots of sleep, walks in nature, massage, or journaling. It will definitely include "white space," scheduled time to do nothing. Spirit enters us only when we've become empty. In this quiet, fertile place of replenishing ourselves, we can hear the call more clearly and move toward it organically, the way a plant moves toward the sun.

> **Without nourishing our own souls, we can't nourish the world; we can't give what we don't have. As we give to our souls, we emanate invisibly and involuntarily the light we have received.**
> **—Marianne Williamson**

You are born with a positive intent to enter fully into life, to live your purpose and give your gifts. A divine impulse yearns to express itself through the creative uniqueness that is you. As we fulfill this internal code to be our authentic selves in all the many colors, styles, and flavors that our uniqueness offers, we feel joyful. As we discover new avenues for our self-expression, we grow, and as we do, we add to the expansion of all that is. Women, inimitable multitaskers that we are, are capable of *conceiving* possibilities for the greater good, as well as *delivering* on those possibilities. As we do, we fulfill our greatest purpose, to know ourselves as creators—conscious architects of our destiny.

> **If we would have life enter into us, we ourselves must enter into life.**
> **—Thomas Troward**

Looking Ahead

As you move through the rest of this chapter, you'll become bolder in taking action on your soul's behalf.

By being true to your soul's intent you will:

- Be empowered to take risks in the "zone of possibility"
- Discover the sweet spot between receptivity and proactivity
- Create alignment between your true values and actions

Stories

You now know that to take inspired action, you need to move beyond the needs of the ego. But how do you listen to the whispers of your soul? How do you find a way to act on your soul's behalf? In the stories you're about to read, you'll learn from three different women who did just that. In fact, each put her masculine go-get-'em side in service to her feminine intuition and benefited from taking inspired action.

Don't look for your dreams to come true, look to become true to your dreams.
—Reverend Michael Beckwith

Lynn's Story: Trusting Soul's Whispers

Lynn's inviting presence suggests an intimacy usually earned after years of friendship. "You're so close to reaching me!" says her playful voice mail message, and you know that you are.

Lynn was well regarded in the business world, especially the printing industry. Her superb sales record meant she could walk into any printing company and they would beg to hire her. She had earned a stellar reputation among peers and customers by making her job her life. Printing presses worked around the clock, and for more than eighteen years so did Lynn. She wore her pager twenty-four hours a day, seven days a week. She prided herself on being able to go days with only a few hours' sleep.

Post–9/11, sales slowed and profits slimmed. The financial rewards Lynn had enjoyed no longer justified her long hours. Feeling restless, she began to investigate different professions that might fulfill her on other levels.

Lynn's incredible bond with her clients was at the heart of her success. She realized that her love of people would be central to anything she did next. Over the next year, drawn by her soul's urgings, she became certified in two different healing techniques. Practicing at the clinic where she earned her certification, Lynn was a natural at coaching people to make positive changes. Her soul felt satisfied, but her practical side couldn't see how this vocation would allow her to maintain her standard of living.

A year later, Lynn took a trip to Bali and was captivated by the country and its people. The beauty, colors, and fragrances replenished her. The Balinese spirit, kindness, and humble reverence for life fed her soul. Like a tight fist slowly opening, Lynn started to relax and return to her own natural rhythms.

After returning to the United States, Lynn began to attend services at a church. She prayed about working in the healing arts, serving others, making good money, and continuing to deepen herself spiritually. One day after the service, a man approached her. "I don't know why I need to meet you, but something tells me I do. Let me introduce myself," he said.

Over coffee, Lynn shared with Greg, a market analyst, that she was trying to figure out her next phase in life. "You should sell your house," he declared. "If you never listen to anything else I tell you, please listen to this. The market has topped out. If you sell now, in five years you can probably buy it back for a lot less."

Lynn had never thought of selling her home, her sanctuary. "But what if I looked at my house like a stock?" she asked herself. "What do you do when you think a stock is at its top? You sell." Lynn was ready to risk her "security" in service of her soul's yearning.

All the real estate professionals she met with agreed: it was a bad time to sell and she should wait until spring. "Then you can put it on the market for high eights or maybe low nines," they told her. But she and her church prayer group were praying for an easy sale and a million-dollar purchase price, so Lynn decided to sell it herself. Drawing upon her skills and ease as a salesperson, Lynn dove into the role of real estate agent. Within a week she had six offers, most over asking price.

People kept asking her, "Where are you moving to? What are you going to do next?" The only answer she had was, "I don't know."

Two day's after Lynn's house sale went through, her best friend, Barb, announced to her, "I'm going to my house in India for a month and you're coming with me." That was all Lynn needed for the moment—the first leg of her journey.

When we act in service of our souls, it invites magic. In saying yes to selling her house and to her friend Barb's invitation, Lynn was moving in the direction of her soul's yearnings. In risking her current identity for a greater purpose, she was in the flow.

The very next week, a colleague called. "Are you sitting down? A man I know is committed to donating $40 million to start healing clinics, educational programs, and retreat centers—starting in the U.S. and going abroad. You're the first person I'm calling. We want you on the team. Just let me know exactly what you'd like to do and how much you'd like to earn and I'll make it happen."

Lynn had responded to the call from her soul and the universe had generously conspired on her behalf. "When I made the decision to let go and follow my heart, *so* much more than I ever imagined happened," she says. "Without a doubt I know that I'm on the right path."

My spirit has become light as a falling leaf. I am learning to trust that which breathes most gently in me.
—Laurel Burch

Emily's Story: The Perils of Perfectionism

Emily was in her early forties when she left her job as manager at a high-tech company to focus on her husband's business and raising a family. A loving mom, she lavished attention on her two girls and teenage stepson while helping her husband, Bob, build a successful company. After seven years of dedication, it was Emily's turn to invest in herself. Bob was happy to reciprocate with his support. Only Emily couldn't seem to make time for writing and sketching—the very things she said she most wanted to do.

We often put our heart's desires on hold with the weak promise of "maybe later." But later had arrived for Emily, and she still wasn't able to grasp the opportunity. Where was Emily's resistance coming from?

Emily told me that, since childhood, she would deliberate endlessly over school reports, collecting data until her mother would finally say, "Just write the report!" This internal pressure to be perfect played into the way she parented, worked, and managed herself. She referred to the part of her that forced her to do things perfectly as the "Battle Ax" and longed to leave it behind. Even with her new creative projects, Emily unwittingly superimposed her old style onto her new endeavor. She pressured herself to be productive—to complete each artistic project, perfectly and on deadline, and to always "make something of it." Emily realized that she wasn't just looking to switch activities. What she really sought was a totally new experience—one of freedom and joy that could only come from within. To transition to this next phase of her life, she had to address who she was *being* on the inside.

We often rush to an outcome by insisting we answer the question, "How can I make a living from this?" To cultivate your unique gifts, you first have to nurture them into being without forcing them to earn their keep. By following your simplest of desires, you tell your inner self, "I believe in you." And even if you have no idea what your "calling" is, you have soul desires—to walk in nature, listen to Mozart, or play your guitar. You'll know it is yours to do if you get "paid" just in the doing of it. When you follow these desires you affirm the deepest part of you. As you become more joyful and lenient about spending time with what you love, your "destined" gifts emerge.

You'll recognize an authentic desire when simply thinking about it whets your appetite. The positive energy it beckons with sweeps away old fears and resistance. Emily was out of practice at following her own passions. She had prioritized others' needs for so long she wasn't even sure what she wanted. But when she talked about writing, she lit up. Although few knew, she had always been able to sit down with pen in hand and spontaneously write stories like they were pouring through her. She could envision an intact play in a dream state and then later capture it on paper.

Both sides of our nature are needed to midwife our creative gifts. It takes soft, gentle reassurance from your kindest heart to coax your core gifts out. At the same time, it requires the muscle of your masculine side to husband your fragile heart's desires, protecting them from invasion by more vocal demands. Previously, Emily had trivialized her writing by referring to it as "just a hobby." Now she established boundaries around her creative time. By naming it her "open and artistic" time, she positively reframed her activity and made a pact to give herself every Friday from noon to two to read, write, or even daydream, as long as she was devoted to her artistic side's whims. She agreed to suspend self-judgment and extend the same respect she might give her own little girls if they were budding artists. The only ground rule was: no Battle Axes allowed!

It takes great discipline to be a free spirit.
—Gabrielle Roth

Exercises

In order to grow beyond the compulsion to please others and instead cultivate our own gifts, two things are necessary: self-affirmation and time. Until we give ourselves the approval and space to follow our needs and desires, we'll keep finding reasons to continue doing what we're good at, even if it no longer fulfills us. The exercises in this section will help you create a safe space to grow.

Inspired Action Audit

Inspired action is the sweet spot between receptivity and proactivity: listening to guidance and actively engaging. Are you white-knuckling the steering wheel of life? Do you have your foot on the gas and the brake at the same time? If your need for control is drowning out your inner guidance, see if you can find a happy medium between thinking it's all up to you and letting the universe drive. There's comfort in knowing that we're held in the hands of a greater force.

For each of the following statements, rate yourself on a scale of 1 to 5, with 1 being "rarely true" and 5 being "usually true."

1. Under stress I tend to procrastinate, "cave in," or withdraw.
2. Under stress I tend to push forward, using sheer will and determination to reach my goal.
3. I stick to my plans no matter what impediments show up.
4. I get easily distracted from what's important and at the end of the day feel frustrated by how little I got done.
5. I can't make myself do what doesn't come naturally.
6. I evaluate myself by how much I produced or accomplished.
7. I typically jump into action without clarifying my priorities.
8. I am more comfortable giving than receiving.
9. I don't voluntarily take risks that make me uncomfortable, even if it seems good for my career or personal life.

We fall out of balance when our attitude is either "whatever!" or conversely, "I'm going to make this happen no matter what!" If half or more of your answers were 4s and 5s, you are over-weighted in either the masculine or the feminine. Select one behavior from the list that you would most like to shift and, using your intuition, see if you are inspired to act in a more balanced way.

White Space

Author Elizabeth Gilbert says that you don't need to gallop the globe to capture an *Eat, Pray, Love* experience. Instead, your journey can start with an internal conversation. She says, "I really feel the one non-negotiable thing you need is to find a tiny little corner of your life, of your day, of stillness where you can begin to ask yourself those burning essential questions of your life. Who am I? Where did I come from? Where am I going? What am I here for?"

It's a revolutionary act to do *inaction* consciously. This week schedule time for stillness by leaving white space in your calendar. Block out two thirty-minute segments for sacred stillness and reflection. Turn off all electronics and take care that you will not be interrupted. Use this time to reconnect with your innermost self however you like—through meditation, journaling, a solo visit in nature, or just resting. Notice how even a short respite is soul renewing and puts you in touch with your greater truth. The paradox is this: intentional action begins with inaction.

Only at rest can we hear what we have not heard before, and be led to what is most deeply beautiful, necessary, and true.

—Wayne Muller

Soul Dialogue

The catalyst to inspired action is often an event that breaks us open. Catalysts like this are not always pleasant, but they open a window for our soul to speak directly to us. You can initiate this same dialogue at any time. In one of your white space practices this week, open your journal, get quiet, and listen to the answers to the following questions:

1. What do I need to let go of?
2. What deep soul promise do I want to be sure to keep?
3. Regarding (current issue or problem), how is my soul telling me to proceed?
4. What action am I inspired to take on behalf of my soul today?

Dreams pass into the reality of action. From the actions stems the dream again; and this interdependence produces the highest form of living.

—Anaïs Nin

Highlights

- We each have a driving need to self-ACTualize—to fulfill our potential.
- Taking inspired action means doing what makes us feel most alive and engaged.
- By integrating our masculine and feminine sides we learn to take actions in alignment with our soul's purpose.
- As Lynn teaches us, there are great rewards in acting on behalf of our soul's whispers.
- Emily shows us how we can overcome perfectionism to pursue our callings.
- To become happier and more successful, make the activities and strengths that light you up a part of your daily life.

The Second Turning

Aspiration

As you enter this next dimension of your evolution there is a profound shift in the way you approach life. The motivation that used to get you up and out of bed in the morning has radically changed. You'll still be checking things off your to-do list, trying to answer your e-mails, moving forward on projects at work, and trying to get dinner on the table, but the reason for your existence no longer stems from self-improvement, trying to be "good," "better than . . . ," or proving yourself in any way.

The First Turning has been emboldening you to live a more authentic life. You are no longer pushing and plodding along the linear path, doing whatever it takes to get somewhere or doing things that merely provide you with what Rabbi Abraham Joshua Heschel called the "forgeries of happiness." You get that the "more" you seek is about living the fullness of each moment, growing from every experience, and joyfully expressing your gifts. No longer a puppet to your moods—or your inherited conditioning from society, parents, or past—you now have the tools to be the conscious designer of your life.

Of course, you're not perfect at it. You may lovingly catch yourself letting circumstances or people dictate how you feel, think, or act. But you relish the newfound power that comes from your moment-to-moment choice to become a fully responsible, conscious co-creator and author of your life. By being, thinking, feeling, speaking, and acting in alignment with your true self, you are saying to the universe, "Bring me a higher life!" And it's on its way.

In this Second Turning, you will move beyond trying to improve yourself to fit some old picture you hold of what a successful woman looks like and instead you will liberate your unique, quirky, even sassy, unabashedly authentic self and bring her to the table.

Sister, you have arrived!

CHAPTER 8

Become a Wide Receiver

The Co-Creative Power of Energy

Every blade of grass has its angel that bends over it and whispers, "Grow, grow."
—**The Talmud**

I once read that a rocket uses 70 percent of its fuel in liftoff. Each time we embark on a new adventure or calling, we must generate a great deal of positive, propulsive, self-affirming energy. It's not always easy to believe in ourselves, especially when at first we see no tangible evidence to validate that we can achieve our ambitions. We may feel vulnerable and insecure. No longer identified with what we were, yet not fully conceiving of what we will become, we are like a seed ripe with creative potential. To bloom into our potential, we must reach deep inside and ignite our inner "yes!" Our first move in this direction is energetic—it requires the Co-Creative Power of Energy.

In the First Turning, you came to know your energy as a Co-Creative Power and discovered that it is possible to change your life just by being deliberate with your energy. You learned ways to boost and replenish yourself so that your energy account stays balanced and full, and how to focus your energy intentionally. Even so, at the first level of the spiral, we often become aware of the energy we're sending only after we've reaped what we've sown—that is, when we get "feedback" from the universe in the form of the people and experiences we attract most often.

In this next turning you will become more skillful with your energy. You will learn how to control and direct it in order to attract the outcomes you desire and to raise the vibration of everyone around you. Simply by attuning to the subtleties of this extraordinary Co-Creative Power, your inner wisdom will become more accessible, you will become more influential, and you'll attract more of what you want.

Everything we think, feel, say, or do creates either an expansive or a contractive energy. Our energy feels best when it's flowing and expanding. Criticism, judgment, and condemnation create contracted energy, while love, charity, kindness, and inspired actions create open, expansive, flowing energy.

The energy *behind* our thoughts, words, feelings, and actions ultimately defines our life experiences. And it is often our response to what comes to us that determines whether we spiral up or down. In the course of a human life we experience many opportunities to expand and contract as we encounter the vicissitudes of winning and losing, illness and health, prosperity and lack. To evolve from an automatic, conditioned life to one that is truly invented and inspired, we must become skillful at being both energetically receptive and intentional, no matter what comes. As we learn to ride the contractions of life and keep our spiral open and flowing, we are carried to our next level of creative self-expression.

Energy from Within

To become more skillful with our energy in the Second Turning, we first shift our reference point from outside of ourselves to inside, from *out* to *in*. For instance, rather than mirroring other people's energy—reacting to them or adjusting ourselves according to what we think they might need or like— we decree how *we* will *be*. We become curious about ourselves, not in a self-absorbed or self-conscious way, but with the receptive energy of an attentive best friend.

Some years ago I had the good fortune of working with the pioneer of sensory awareness, Charlotte Selver. This radiant woman, who was still teaching at one hundred years of age, taught me about my capacity for self-renewal by engaging with the newness of every moment. Her workshops consisted of students lying on the floor and making conscious micro-movements with our bodies, solely when we felt the energetic impulse to do so. Charlotte pointed out that we are usually so goal-oriented in our actions that we've lost the sense of what it is like to *approach* and *arrive*. She instructed us to raise one leg and then place it on the floor. We did this repeatedly. At first, my experience was somewhat mechanical—lifting and dropping my leg to the floor. As I became more present to each sensation and each unique impulse to move, my awareness heightened. Time slowed, and I felt the weight of my muscles and the fabric of my jeans against my skin. I wasn't moving anymore as if I were pulling the strings of a puppet; I now felt *inside* of each moment.

We were being trained to orient ourselves from a place deeper than our minds. As I dropped into the subtle sensations of movement and stillness, my thoughts faded and I felt more alive. As I became more *internally* referenced, orienting from the inside out, I felt a sense of oneness with each movement, with myself, and with everyone and everything else around me. This was a startling contrast to my day-to-day existence, where my actions were habitually reactive—driven by the past or the future. Through Charlotte's practice, I discovered *me*, not as my thinking mind, but as pure awareness—pure energy.

Choosing to Open

When the shutters are closed, the sunlight cannot get in.
—Eckhart Tolle

After we shift our focus from the world outside us to the world within, we make the second energetic shift—from *closed* to *open*. By compassionately listening to the wisdom of our energy, we let it circulate! By meeting ourselves wherever our energy state is, we allow our energy to return to its natural, open state where we are vibrant, spacious, and flowing. This is the energy that asks us, "What would love do now?"

The light of universal energy already flows through us. Our task is to choose to align again and again with this loving essence—our true self. This essence knows that we are perfect and that we are meant to live our fullest expression in life.

When we are kind and loving, especially to ourselves, we take advantage of the Co-Creative Power of Energy to its fullest. We become what my friend Susan Greene calls our own wide receiver of life. When our energy is open and expansive, we are fully present in our bodies. Alert and awake to life, we are more available to life's endless stream of miracles—the serendipitous connections and timely messages that guide us on our way. Attuned to both our inner state and what is happening in the moment, we make wiser choices and depend less on external things to fulfill us.

Being open also has its challenges. As we become more aware of the atmosphere of people and places, we may need to be more selective in what we partake of. We don't have to stay tuned to every program being broadcast. But we can regularly ask ourselves, "What energy am I sensing here?" Or if we suddenly feel an energetic rigidity or contraction, we can ask ourselves, "What am I tuned to that triggered my reaction?"

It's only our resistance to life—other people's behavior, a situation, our own thoughts—that causes our energy to contract. Without a transformation of consciousness, our default is to let life's pressures and difficulties close our energy down. This inner "no" can be in reaction to a traffic jam, a person's attitude, our body's limitations, or life in general. But it is within our power to shift from this stressed-out closed state to the energy of compassionate acceptance—a heartfelt inner "yes."

Opening to Receive

We regularly receive messages from our energy body—it serves as a barometer for how well our needs are getting met. Not just our physical needs, but our emotional needs and our soul's needs as well. If our energy drops, it is likely that we need to attend to some need. Negative energy arises when we resist our needs for rest, emotional connection, or fun, or when we are posturing against whatever is happening in the moment.

You've heard the saying "What we resist persists"? Resistance to what *is* causes contraction, whereas acceptance and cooperation cause expansion. This truism is best illustrated by martial arts masters. When they engage with opponents, rather than physically obstructing them, they *receive them* and then step aside, allowing the force of the oncoming assailants to propel them on their way. They know that if they oppose a force they have to add energy, but if they receive it and allow it to flow by, the energy dissipates.

The key to transforming our consciousness is to remain open to experience without condemnation or judgment. As we go through our day, we catch any constraints in our energy, like a minor tightening in the stomach or a vague feeling that something bad is about to happen. And then, instead of letting a twinge turn into an energy leak (a bad habit or destructive pattern), we take it as a cue, lean into it, observe it, and see if we can be informed by its message.

When we tenderly move *toward* distress, rather than away, we give it space to move. Being open to painful experiences as well as pleasurable ones is central to mastering the Co-Creative Power of Energy. This attentiveness to the fluctuations in our energy really pays off when we listen to and follow through on our wisdom's message. When we do more of what expands our energy and less of what constrains it, our energy lifts.

> **It is only as we allow the Divine current to flow through us, in and out, we really express life.**
> —**Ernest Holmes**

Looking Ahead

In this chapter, you will learn how to shape and silently broadcast your inner state of being as conscious, open, and radiant energy. By becoming a wide receiver, you will:

- Realize that you have a choice about the energy you send to others
- Be inspired to shift your energy in ways that positively affect situations
- Learn to receive messages from your energy to guide you on your path
- Become skilled at tuning in to your energy and what you need to keep it flowing

Stories

We all know what it feels like to be sucked into a downward spiral—to wake at three in the morning stuck in an energy pattern that makes us suffer. The following stories offer firsthand accounts of women who discovered how the deliberate use of energy produces a positive and tangible reciprocal effect. Imagine what could happen for you if you became open to loving, flowing energy even in the face of adversity.

Sharon's Story: It Just Takes One

We've all been in a situation where, out of fear, we find ourselves running on ego and trying to control everyone and everything. Sharon, a vice president at a large entertainment company, was vying to take charge of a high-visibility project. She felt that Beth, another vice president, had tried to undermine her in front of the CEO in an attempt to win the project. Sharon was especially frustrated because the project's success depended on collaboration.

Lying in bed at night, Sharon would compulsively recycle things she wanted to say or strategies she could employ to stay in control. Her energy became tight and fearful as her thoughts churned like hamsters on a wheel. Even though some part of Sharon was desperate to escape the grip the situation seemed to have on her, she couldn't seem to let go.

"I have to watch my back. This woman is out to get me," Sharon declared during one of our coaching sessions.

"If you go on like this, she'll succeed," I replied. "You've got to try something different."

It only takes one person to shift the energy dynamic between two people. With some prodding from me and with the added pressure of her boss's presence at the meeting, Sharon decided to temporarily suspend her suspicions and try a fresh and courageous approach. Instead of matching what she perceived as Beth's adversarial energy by being manipulative and controlling, she genuinely offered compassionate, supportive energy by publicly acknowledging Beth for her part on the project and inviting her input. Beth looked surprised, but her body language visibly softened and relaxed. There was a noticeable shift in Beth's energy from cold and polite to friendly and warm. From that point on, they became each other's advocates.

Dianne's Story: A Positive Shift

Dianne was annoyed because Kate, the Human Resources representative for the company she was interviewing with, arrived late for their meeting. Kate didn't have the proper paperwork and made no apologies for having to reschedule. When Dianne and I spoke about it later, her attitude was to "wait and see" if she was still interested in the opportunity based on Kate's "professionalism" next time they met.

Having already worked with me through the First Turning, Dianne was aware of her tendency to be judgmental. She also knew deep down that we never really know why people act the way they do. In retrospect, Dianne realized there could have been lots of reasons that Kate was so disorganized. Perhaps Kate had an argument with her husband that morning or got a speeding ticket on her way to work. After doing some discreet checking to make sure that Kate's somewhat scattered energy wasn't the product of working in an overachieving, unrelenting environment—one that she herself wouldn't want to join—Dianne decided that she would be proactive by shifting her own energy. She wanted to experience the power of offering a more positive, open energy, not just for her own sake, but to potentially shift the outcome of the interview.

I suggested that at their next meeting, Dianne think of Kate as a friend who had been through a tough time. As Kate walked into the room, she made a self-deprecating remark about her ever-changing calendar. Dianne smiled compassionately and commented about the unbelievable pace that is the new normal. As the interview progressed, instead of being focused on herself or on what wasn't perfect in the situation, Dianne continued to extend genuine warmth and interest. Kate reciprocated, sharing that for her, as a newly single mom, one of the company's selling points was its child-care facility. Walking out, Dianne realized that, regardless of the outcome, the interview had been a success. She had shown up as who she wanted to be. Three weeks later she was offered the job.

Exercises

Assuming responsibility for the quality of energy we want to experience, we can draw upon our generosity of spirit; we can give people the benefit of the doubt and lift both ourselves and others up. The exercises that follow will help you tune in to your energy at an ever more nuanced level so that it becomes easier to stay open even when you're angry or afraid.

Becoming a Wide Receiver

Every day we are offered numerous invitations to open up or shut down. Learning to consciously shift our vibration from closed to open, from fear to love, causes an instantaneous, positive chain reaction in our lives. Sensing when we are energetically closed—how we block energy or freeze it, how we tense up our bodies and minds—is the first step in opening up. Simply by becoming nonjudgmentally aware of our energy, we begin to shift. Every time we are tempted to harden but choose to reopen and be the bright light that we are, we gain personal power and cause our own happiness.

You can shift your energy just by feeling your nonverbal experience and becoming aware of your body's subtle energy. Ask yourself these three questions now:

Am I open or closed?
Is my breathing shallow or full?
Am I armored in my stomach, tight in my shoulders or chest, or loose and relaxed?

After answering each question, go deeper to describe the energetic feeling in your body in more detail, for example: spacious, calm, heavy, agitated.

After taking this inner inventory, notice whether your body settles and opens. With practice you will become a "wide receiver" to your energy and become more present to the gift of your life.

Listening to Your Body's Wisdom

Our bodies hold so much wisdom; our cells have eons of experience to tap into. It's yours for the asking! When you ask for guidance, you may hear a one-word reply like "Rest." But expect the unexpected. Your body's wisdom can surprise you with profound messages.

The next time your energy or mood feels low, connect to the place in your body where it seems to originate and gently ask:

What is my energy trying to tell me? Examples: slow down, this doesn't feel safe, stop what you're doing, say yes to this.

Then ask, what do I need? Examples: rest, to disengage, appreciation, to start over. Honor your body-mind by taking one action on behalf of your energy's wisdom.

> Discover the resistance that you hold in your body, mind, and heart... then *lean into it.*
>
> —Unknown

Motion or Rest Practice

Life is always expanding or contracting, but sometimes the pulsation gets stuck and our energy needs a jumpstart to flow again. The most important thing to remember is to keep our energy moving. Circulation and flow is health; stagnation and too much concentration is dis-ease. It is the alternation between challenge and rest that keeps us growing and flowing.

Whenever your energy gets stuck, tune in to whether you need rest or motion and do one of the following practices to get it flowing again:

Rest, take a power nap or some quiet time, gaze at a tree outside the window, or listen to some beautiful music.

Or go for a walk, a run, dance, or work out with weights.

While these might seem simple solutions to your energy crisis, they are not. Responding to stuck energy by resting or getting into motion is a radical departure from the work "norm" that tells us to buckle down and remain at our desks and computers, no matter what. Paradoxically, by taking breaks you will lift your energy and get more done.

Highlights

- Resistance to "what is" causes our energy to contract.
- Claim your personal power by regularly shifting your energy from closed to open, and from out to in.
- As Sharon's story illustrates, it only takes one person to shift the energy dynamic between two people.
- Ego feeds on the energy of fear and scarcity.
- Your body's wisdom can surprise you with profound messages.
- To find the rhythm and wisdom of your true energy, you must slow down.

CHAPTER 9

Untie Your Limiting kNOTS

The Co-Creative Power of Mind

**I am an old man and have known a great many troubles,
but most of them never happened.**
—oft-attributed to Mark Twain

A Cherokee elder was teaching his grandchildren about life. He said to them, "A fight is going on inside me. It is a terrible fight and it is between two wolves.

"One wolf represents fear, anger, envy, sorrow, regret, greed, arrogance, self-pity, guilt, resentment, inferiority, lies, false pride, superiority, and ego. The other stands for joy, peace, love, hope, sharing, serenity, humility, kindness, benevolence, friendship, empathy, generosity, truth, compassion, and faith. This same fight is going on inside you, and inside every other person, too."

The grandchildren thought about it for a minute, and then one child asked his grandfather, "Which wolf will win?"

The old Cherokee replied simply, "The one I feed."

Life is filled with paradox: praise and blame, gain and loss, pleasure and pain. Within each of us is the capacity for creating heaven or hell. Working with the Co-Creative Power of Mind at this level will help you remember, as this famous story reminds us, that in every moment the choice is up to us.

Creating a Healthy Mind

Our body's innate ability to maintain health is based on three simple principles: circulation, assimilation, and elimination. The prescription for mental health is the same. Thoughts are meant to circulate and flow, just like everything that is healthy.

When we are present in the moment, we can observe our thoughts scrolling by like a ticker tape, an endless stream of ever-changing commentary. If we're judging ourselves, our outlook will reflect the volatility of our personal "stock" in its upward and downward spikes. "That was a good move. I'm smart!" we say. Days or even moments later, our stock plummets: "I'm an idiot!" Author Robert Bly names one side of our seemingly split personality The Grandiose One and the other, her twin, Utter Worthlessness. But this isn't who we are. It's only when we take either side too seriously—when we stop observing the thoughts and start identifying with them—that we get into trouble.

Circulation is what keeps things flowing; assimilation is taking in what is nourishing; and elimination is releasing what is not. Just as our bodies assimilate nutrients and expel the rest, we support our psyche's well-being when we welcome or *receive* all our thoughts and experiences, and discard or *release* what doesn't serve us.

Choosing What You Feed

Much of the time, life goes merrily along until something happens that conflicts with the way we think things should be, sending us into a downward spiral. *She* gets the promotion we want, *he* doesn't call, *we* get a diagnosis. With little or no warning, we find ourselves in a mind storm of upsetting thoughts insisting that we've been offended, rejected, or dealt an unfair hand. We don't decide to have these thoughts; they just seem to show up and spiral us down.

Without conscious awareness, we don't filter out these unsavory thoughts. Instead, we invite them to pull up a chair and stay awhile. *I'm a failure. She's stuck-up. It's too hard.* When we feed our judgments, fears, and loathing in this way, they grow strong.

Negative stories of any kind, about us or anyone else, get us into a kNOT of mental suffering. A kNOT is the result of our resistance to what is—an argument with reality, an invalidation of ourselves. When we bring our full attention to the now, more often than not there is nothing wrong in that moment. Byron Katie asks the provocative question, "Who would you be without your story?" Every time you drop into the fullness of the moment, you build a stronger connection to the calm, deep intelligence that is the birthplace of your intuition, wisdom, and creative action. Returning from being lost in thought to the felt sense of the moment, you create a tiny space in your train of thoughts and your consciousness brightens. Doing this repeatedly over time develops a quality of presence also known as charisma: the attractive aura that magnetizes the ideal people and opportunities to you. The goal is therefore to become more discriminating about which thoughts you choose to dwell upon and to return to the present moment again and again.

A "thought" is different from "thinking." We're all subject to the endless commentary about what we like, don't like, agree with, or are threatened by, ad infinitum. Thoughts become thinking when we energize a thought through attention, making it stronger and more developed. Emotionally charged thinking, invested in repeatedly and over time, becomes a belief. Sheer repetition etches a groove in our brains, so a thought stream that began as a trickling brook becomes a gushing river hungrily fed by tributaries of similar thoughts.

As we learn to detach from our ever-changing stream of thoughts and get intentional about which ones we empower, we transform. When we realize that every experience is for our evolution, even uncomfortable thoughts carry gifts. If you believed that each situation was here to teach you a valuable lesson meant to shape you into your most whole and authentic self, would you be more curious about a thought that kNOTs you?

When a thought comes along that ties us in "kNOTs," it may be showing us where our soul wants to expand. By receiving it—but not believing it, accepting it rather than rejecting it, and inquiring into it but not identifying with it—we allow the thought to lighten and move on its way.

Who's Talking to You?

We have a committee of voices in our heads (our inner judge, adolescent, victim, cheerleader, and so on). Because these voices influence us, it behooves us to know which one is talking at any given time. The loudest voice is typically the false self, or *conditioned mind*, which, although it may seem comfortable because it's familiar, can deter us from making a meaningful change in the direction of our dreams.

Luckily, there is a distinct difference in the way the true and false selves speak. Become aware of these nuances and it will be that much easier to decide whether you'll take what they say to heart or not.

The true self's voice often floats in when we're meditating, out in nature, waking from a dream, washing the dishes, or engaged in a repetitive task like showering, gardening, or sweeping. It is usually a softer voice than the commanding voice of the false self, which often makes demands that start with, "You should..." or "You need to..."

If the voice is heavy, urgent, threatening, fearful, resentful, arrogant, defensive, insecure, suspicious, or pejorative in any way—critical, sarcastic, or demeaning— it is the *false* or *incomplete* self. If the voice is smiling, light, kind, certain, compassionate, matter-of-fact, empathic, encouraging, curious, accepting, open, positive, generous, optimistic, eager, inspiring, or confident, it is the *true self.*

Distinguishing between the two voices will help you turn up the volume on the voice of your true self—your inner authority—and provide you with positive guidance to follow your true purpose.

A quick way to determine if the voice is *friend* or *foe* is to sense its color. If it is dark and foreboding, it is the false self; if it is light, calm, and compassionate, it is the true self. The next time you catch the tail end of your own inner commentary, consider the source!

True Self	False Self
Quiets you	Hurries you
Uplifts you	Attacks you
Guides you	Misleads you
Encourages you	Doubts you
Invites you	Commands you
Assures you	Criticizes you
Soothes you	Agitates you

Refocusing with Intention

The more intentional we are with every part of our lives, the more consciously we live. So much depends on our focus.

A friend told me about some rare footage she had seen of two marines running for cover in a combat zone. As they tried to escape the gunfire, one of the soldiers kept looking back to see where his attackers were firing from. Ninety percent of his attention was behind him. The other soldier had all of his attention on swiftly navigating every obstacle to reach the safety of the bunker. He was the one who made it.

Whenever our thoughts stray to the past or future, we put ourselves at risk, not only for physical mishaps but also for unhappiness. An article in *Science* titled "A Wandering Mind Is an Unhappy Mind," by Matthew Killingsworth and Daniel Gilbert, cited data establishing that when we succumb to the worries of the wandering mind, happiness is diminished. Here's the kicker: their research showed that our minds wander almost half the time! It turns out that mindfulness, or being fully present with whatever we're doing, is even more important to our happiness than *what* we're doing. One of the researchers, Dr. Daniel Gilbert said, "Our data suggests that the location of the body is much less important than the location of the mind . . . The heart goes where the head takes it, and neither cares much about the whereabouts of the feet."

When we're not focused, we tend to worry. The word *worry* comes from the Old English *wyrgan*, meaning "to strangle." Fretfulness constricts the flow of divine intelligence that wants to move through us. But it's not our fault. Our brains are hardwired from our hunter–gatherer days to be on the alert for danger. On the Serengeti, making it through to the next day depended on our ability to sense threat. But even in today's world free of saber-toothed tigers ready to pounce, our brains are inclined to worry. Built into our survival-oriented nervous system is a bias to fixate on the negative and to see threats that aren't there. It plays out in our everyday lives as we scan our inner and outer environments for causes of concern. The good news is that once we realize that our brain's default setting of apprehension is usually not based in reality, we can take those fear thoughts less seriously and put our attention elsewhere.

When you remove your attention from thoughts that don't serve you, where do you place it instead? The best answer is the present moment. Notice the tree outside your window; feel the texture of the paper as you turn the page; or notice the contrast of the letters on the screen. As you breathe in, notice the coolness in your nostrils, feel your lungs expand. Fears and worries almost always arise when we're captured by thoughts about the past or the future. By returning to the present, we move out of the cacophony of mental traffic and into the calm of the now.

The quality and direction of our intentional focus can also play a pivotal role in realizing our dreams. Whatever you *attend to* gets energized and magnified, whether it's something you want or something you don't. Your focus sets up a magnetic resonance that attracts similar or like energy experiences. Success coach and *Chicken Soup for the Soul* author Jack Canfield points out that when we set our sights on something, we open the filter of our reticular activating system (RAS), the brain function that sorts incoming stimuli. We start to notice resources and solutions that may have been in our environment all along: books, strategies, ways to raise money, even people who can help us achieve our goal.

Fortunately, the idea that our thoughts shape our reality has finally reached the mainstream. Many have realized that focusing on their desires can greatly enhance their lives. Have you noticed the popularity of "life lists"? Once the domain of college grads, people at career crossroads, or those reinventing their lives, today these "things to do before I die" lists are as common as grocery lists.

Many goal setters, though, are focused on "what not to do"—what they don't want—rather than what they are called to do or who they are called to be. Losing weight ranks first in popularity on New Year's resolutions. But this form of negative intention can backfire because it works to confirm our perceived past failures and reinforce our negative self-image. This applies to many situations, including our professional lives. For example, how many of us, when considering a career change, tend to focus on the horrors we're currently facing and how we feel about *not* having our ideal work situation? We get pulled into thinking what a bummer it is that we aren't where we "should" be and conclude that there is something wrong with us that we haven't made it happen yet. The result? We cease to be a magnet for what we truly desire.

So how do you set and manifest a powerful, heart-driven intention? Instead of writing down "lose twenty pounds," think about framing it this way: "Today I will celebrate my body and do one thing to make it feel more healthy and fit." If you intend to find a more fulfilling job, try fixing your attention on what that job might be, how inspiring it will be to do what you love, and how you will feel when you have it.

Do you see how different that is? It's subtle, but if our intentions are going to inspire us to live joyously, how we state them and how we feel when we think about them are as important as the intentions themselves.

When you feel a longing, it's a message from your soul reminding you what you really want. Setting a powerful "intention" (from the Latin *intento*, "to stretch toward") is a surefire method of stretching the mind wide enough to accept your highest good.

Looking Ahead

We create our current and future reality thought by thought. Thoughts of cynicism, resentment, or vindication might still come calling. But we have a way of dealing with them. We don't have to bolt the door or give them free access to our minds.

By receiving, releasing, and refocusing, you'll become skilled at managing your mind as you learn to:

- Distinguish the thoughts of your false self from those of your true self
- *Receive* your highest wisdom
- Identify and *release* thoughts that are stopping you
- *Focus* on the intentions that bring you and your vision alive

As you become increasingly skilled at this process, you will be reminded of the truth about you—that you are filled with infinite possibilities.

> **Those who do not have power over the story that dominates their lives, the power to retell it, rethink it, deconstruct it…and change it as times change, truly are powerless.**
>
> **—Salman Rushdie**

Stories

Whenever an unwanted situation keeps recurring, it can be a clue that unconscious beliefs are working at cross-purposes with what we say we want. However, just as it's more difficult to eliminate a bad habit than it is to replace it with a positive one, so it goes with our beliefs. Our limiting beliefs are almost certain to prevail unless we replace them with more conscious and heartfelt intentions. The following stories tell about two women who let go of self-defeating mind-sets to realign with their higher aspirations.

Chantal's Story: Outing Our Buried Beliefs

In our first meeting, Chantal, an articulate professional and mother of two, expressed frustration about her boss: "This isn't the first time I've been passed over for a promotion." Her anger bubbled just beneath the surface as she recounted how unfair it was that she wasn't offered opportunities: "They continually go to guys less equipped than I am to do the job."

Losing out on a recent promotion had left Chantal feeling undervalued and unappreciated. Her quandary was that she had always received positive performance reviews and never any direct feedback that would explain what she called a stalled career.

An important clue that counterproductive thoughts were festering was Chantal's victim mind-set. When something unexpected and unpleasant happens, it's easy to think that it's happening *to* us. But no matter how true it seems, the "woe-is-me" mind-set is not a powerful place from which to make a change. I was eager to support Chantal in eliminating the thoughts that might be playing a part in sabotaging her career.

We took a closer look to see if there was a correlation between her self-image and the unwanted situation. "Chantal," I asked, "could *not* being acknowledged for your gifts somehow fit with what you think or fear about who you are?" Looking away sheepishly she said, "I've always believed that there was something lacking in me—that I had a hole in my soul."

"The feeling that something is wrong with you is not a personal belief," I reassured her. "It's a collective one." In truth, I was familiar with this feeling of lack myself, and I had heard endless variations on it from clients. Sometimes it took the form of another burdensome outlook: "I'm better than you." Both originate from the illusion that we're separate from our source, a hallmark of the small self. Either way our ego spins it, inferiority or grandiosity, it is an ungrounded self-assessment.

Knowing that there is a universal perfection in the way things are, I asked Chantal, "How is your current job meeting an important need of yours?" She admitted that it afforded her the ear of her boss's boss and other senior leaders. A part of Chantal was satisfied with this arrangement, even without equitable pay or title, because of the special status it afforded her. Her small self's need to feel "special" superseded her higher intention to advance her career.

Chantal also realized that she harbored a fear (a supercharged thought) that more responsibility would mean sacrificing time with her children. True or not, this served as another counterintention working against her.

We may think we're fully committed to achieving or acquiring something we want, but if it just isn't happening, the universe may be responding to a different message we're simultaneously sending. Until we "out" any buried beliefs that run contrary to our declared desire, we'll stay stuck where we are.

Although Chantal's counter-intentions were invisible to her, they created and communicated a huge STOP sign to the universe, canceling out her intention for a promotion. By becoming aware of and questioning her thoughts, she received and released her subterranean beliefs, liberating herself from a dysfunctional pattern. She made an Inner Vow that read: "I am whole and complete. I engage in life with dignity and grace." With this new internal reference point, Chantal chose to seek a new job within her company—not out of anger or reactivity, but in a spirit of responsibility. She could see that her former job was somehow a fit with who she used to be, but it no longer served who she was becoming. Chantal had shifted her focus from lack to fullness, from "I'm not" to "I am," and become her own self-replenishing fountain.

Life tangibly changes when we grow ourselves. As Chantal's consciousness evolved, the universe responded with new circumstances. Within a very short time an opportunity popped up with a female leader, Judith, whom Chantal had always admired. More importantly, in her appreciation of Chantal's talents, Judith mirrored Chantal's newfound self-respect.

When we believe our thoughts, we suffer. But when we question them, we don't suffer. Freedom is as simple as that!

—Byron Katie

Kelly's Story: Confronting the Commander

Kelly, a charismatic, outgoing trainer with a Fortune 500 company, worked seventy hours a week. When she was able to take a break on the weekends, she was too tired to do anything but veg out in front of the TV and eat fast food. She was gaining weight and felt exhausted, but didn't know how she could unplug from her relentless schedule. As we worked together, she gradually learned to put *herself*, instead of her *work*, at the center of her life by saying yes to her true self's quieter needs. And her world started to change for the better. Yet there was still more inner excavation needed for Kelly to break some hardened habits. We can tell ourselves we want to do something differently, but until we engage with the deeper sources of our resistance, nothing changes.

One of the most powerful turnaround exercises for Kelly was a dialogue between what she called her *Commander* (false self) and her *Spirit* (true self). This negotiation freed her from blind obedience to her fear-based taskmaster (the ego/false self) and turned up the volume on the voice of her emerging conscious self.

Commander: You've stopped putting in overtime! You are slacking off and you will fail!

Spirit: I will not work so late that I am completely exhausted, arriving home just in time to go to bed and nothing else.

I suggested to Kelly that she ask her Spirit what she wanted instead.

Spirit: I want to leave at a more reasonable hour so that I still have some time for myself each evening.

Commander: Well, that's nice, but you're always way behind. How do you expect to stay on top of your workload?

Spirit: I realize I'm behind. I will commit to some time on the weekend when needed, but I will not work an entire weekend. Everything doesn't have to be so perfect!

Commander: I'm just trying to help you be successful. This is the way you've always done it, and look how many years you've kept this job!

I pointed out that our egos (in this case Kelly's Commander) originally formed from a positive intention to protect us from some perceived danger. Very often, the part of us that feels like a drill sergeant is born of a good intention—to keep us safe. Appreciating that good intention, without succumbing to its demands, makes it possible to work out a happy compromise. I suggested that she thank the Commander for his help and ask if he would be willing to be redeployed to a new assignment. For instance, someone with his "taskmaster" strengths could remind her to leave work on time or insist that she get to bed early to get enough sleep.

Spirit: Thank you for everything you have done to make me successful. But if I don't allow time to do some things that are solely for me, I won't be around to be successful. Since you're so good at reminding me about things, could you help me take better care of myself?

Commander: If you made a concerted effort to get to bed a bit earlier, it would ensure a solid night's sleep, and you would be more effective.

Spirit: Yes. I think that is a great start! Thank you.

Exercises

Unearthing the beliefs that drive us at an unconscious level—and engaging them in a frank dialogue—can be a relief, a revelation, and a huge liberation. It's also hard work. The exercises here offer some tools to start digging and some guidelines to start clearing.

Untie Your kNOTs

When we declare a bold vision or intention that is worthy of us, it can call up kNOTs in the form of limiting beliefs. These don't surface to torture us; they come up to be refuted so that we can realize more wholeness. The beliefs that arise are usually the same ones that have prevented us from having what we wanted in the past. What a great opportunity to heal and dissolve anything that kNOTs us!

Now, in the Second Turning, we're unearthing and dismantling these unconscious impediments to our calling. It will be up to you whether to remain loyal to a belief or call its bluff by inviting forth a more empowered truth.

For example: What do you think would bring you the most happiness?

If you knew you could not fail, what would you undertake to accomplish? What is one major goal for your life?

Now ask yourself, what circumstances do you believe prevent you from realizing these dreams? Examples: enough money, an understanding boss, sufficient self-confidence, a supportive partner. Complete the following statement:

I could have _____ (desired outcome), if only I had _____ (limiting belief).

Now play what I call the "angel's advocate." Take each limiting belief you identified and turn it around or refute it. Build the case for why you are fully capable of manifesting your vision. For example:

Counter: If only I were more connected I could start my own business.

With: I have great relationship skills to help me build a network of connections.

Counter: If only I was financially savvy I could own my own home.

With: Women with fewer resources have accomplished amazing things.

> **Find the places where your beliefs are distorting your vision, and peel away those thoughts like the ill-fitting Clark Kent eyewear they are.**
>
> **—Martha Beck**

Powerful Intention

We've talked about the power of intention to co-create your life and the importance of knowing what you're attracting, consciously or not. This exercise will help you focus on an intention and bring it to life.

Begin by getting clear on one primary intention you want to manifest in the next four weeks. It can be as simple as being more confident, closing a business deal, spending more time with family, or finding your dream job.

Dreams taken too seriously become reality.
                    —Massachusetts Turnpike billboard

Now it's time to visualize—and "feelize"—to realize your intention. Olympic athletes, concert musicians, and accomplished professionals incorporate the power of visualization to manifest their vision. They picture, step by step, how they will perform and what the outcome will be. For an extra edge, try this: imagine both the mental *and* the emotional equivalent of your intention. How will you feel when you have it?

Anticipating emotionally what your intention will feel like when you have it is even more important than mentally rehearsing how you will get there. Revisit that experience frequently. Allow the feeling to monopolize your attention. At the same time, release it to the universe, make room for grace to work in your life, and wait in calm expectancy for your new experience to arrive!

When you broadcast such an intention, there's very little else you have to do.
                    —Srikumar Rao, PhD

See, feel, and sense your own intention now. For the next four questions, come up with three or more answers.

How do I feel when I have it? Examples: peaceful, joyous, proud, hopeful, etc.

What do I see when I have it? Depending on your intention, your answers will vary dramatically. Examples: testimonials from satisfied clients, my bank statement showing a balance of $_____, happy faces around the table, the view from the Eiffel Tower, etc.

Who else is smiling once I have my intention? Examples: my mom, my business partner, children with diabetes, etc.

When my intention is realized, what is different about me? Examples: I am authentic, I am more free-spirited, I am in a loving relationship, etc.

As you reflect on your answers, think about how, by realizing your intention, you not only rise on your own path but also inspire and spread joy to those around you.

Consider the Source!

Recall the characteristics of the true self's voice: soft, matter-of-fact, encouraging, curious, and open, versus the false self's voice, which is urgent, critical, and demanding. Being able to distinguish between these two voices is a huge first step. To take it to the next level, when you sense the voice of your false self: don't believe it! Instead, turn up the volume on your true self. Be encouraging, optimistic, and kind.

When you refuse to see the negative things, they will disappear, and you will be surprised to see how you will change.

—Charles Fillmore

Highlights

- The principles for a healthy body (circulation, assimilation, and elimination) are similar to the principles for a healthy mind: receive, release, and refocus our thoughts.
- You can choose to be happy or unhappy by the thoughts you "feed" yourself.
- Kelly's story shows us that by refereeing the different voices in our head we can resolve inner conflict.
- You can untie your kNOTs by questioning your assumptions and beliefs.
- You realize your intentions by focusing on what you want rather than what you don't want (or don't have).

CHAPTER 10

Trust in Your Awes and Ows

The Co-Creative Power of Feelings

Let everything happen to you.
Beauty and terror.
Just keep going.
No feeling is final.

—Rainer Maria Rilke

In the year after my lupus diagnosis, I felt like a victim. I talked about my troubles to anyone who would listen. "I can't believe I got this. I'm in constant pain. What should I do?" One day, as we drove across the Golden Gate Bridge, my friend Barbara said, "If you keep talking about this all the time, no one will want to be around you." The truth of her words stung. I wanted to defend myself, but I sensed the value of her message.

I had been broadcasting my feelings to others as if those feelings were a hot potato, something I could toss away by talking about them. Instead of proffering sympathy, Barbara responded with a clear boundary, forcing me off my pity pot. Which is just what my soul desired.

Until *I* received and owned my feelings, I couldn't take responsibility for my situation or begin to take practical steps to help myself. More importantly, my soul had a lesson for me that could only be received through my heart. As I let my feelings *in* and worked with them, I slowly began to trust that I could live with my condition—through it, and beyond it—and include it in who I was.

Our Inner Teachers

Feelings are not "the truth," but they are portals to our truth. If you recall a time when you experienced heightened feelings, whether it was for a child, a romantic partner, a place of natural beauty, or an act of kindness or bravery, you likely recall experiencing an intense aliveness—a sense of being in touch with yourself and what mattered.

These are "awe" moments, when we sense the infinite grace behind all things. Krista Tippett, author of *Speaking of Faith*, writes, "The ancient Celts spoke of 'thin places' and 'thin times,' when the veil between heaven and earth is worn thin, where the temporal and the transcendent seem to touch." These moments remind us of the greater story of our lives, offering clues to our values, our purpose, and what we love.

There is a natural rhythm inherent in life that supports our evolution. On a daily basis we are being called to Spiral Up!, not just through the "awes" but also through what I call the "ows": in other words, through moments of joy and pain that insistently point to what we love and what needs to heal. While the moments of joy expand us, the painful passages can make us want to contract and crumble. Those inevitable human experiences of loss and adversity shape us into who we are by how we deal with them. Through them we are invited to be our braver, stronger, and more high-minded selves.

In this way, our hearts are our inner teachers. As we use experiences to become wiser, gentler, and kinder, we make an evolutionary leap. Instead of focusing on the triggering event, and either stuffing or spewing our emotions, we get curious about the feelings they elicit and tease our feelings apart for what they are asking or telling us on a deeper, spiritual level. What might our pain be asking us to outgrow or step into? What is it reminding us of that we really want or care about? What need or passion is it unearthing that we could do something about?

If you have a soul commitment to live an authentic life, the universe will continually coax you to return to the truth by offering experiences that ask you to get real. Our awes and ows come in quiet whispers, then little pinches, and if we still don't listen, they come in the form of a traumatic event or loss that shakes us to our core.

When the Going Gets Hot

The actor Dustin Hoffman compares our pain avoidance reflex to sitting on a radiator. When it gets hot, we jump off. In life, when we bump up against "hot" things in ourselves, like fear, grief, hatred, or jealousy, we automatically pull back. Hoffman explains that acting requires one to dive right into those intense feelings. Likewise, to expand into the person we know we're meant to be, we must learn how to remain present when things heat up. If we don't, we'll keep getting "pinched" until they build up to an ow we can't ignore.

Marisa, who returned to the dating scene after her twenty-year marriage ended, found herself engaged in conversation with an attractive guy as she stood in line at Starbucks. As they were going their separate ways, just when she sensed he was about to ask her for her phone number, she blurted out, "It was great meeting you!" and waved good-bye. Driving away in her car she mentally kicked herself: "Why did I bolt?" A radiator moment.

Territory that initially warns us off with imaginary "Caution, Danger!" signs can often turn out to be the frontier of new ground to claim. When we treat everything in our lives as if it's here for a reason, our emotions become treasures to unearth. By reclaiming marginalized feelings and aspects of ourselves, we discover hidden gifts that can transform our lives.

No matter what is laid before us—regal mountains, deep love from a friend, or all the riches in China—if our hearts are closed, we will not receive the blessings. As we open to what the Buddhists call life's ten thousand joys and ten thousand sorrows, our heart unclenches. As we receive what life presents to us and give generously of the riches within us, we come to know an incandescent joy and a peace beyond our imagination. Pierced by pain, we become permeable to awe. All the holes make us holy.

Stories We Tell Ourselves

Often, when we allow ourselves to delve into painful feelings, we discover a theme running through the ows. That's what happened to me some years ago. With a heart heavy from a breakup, I sought the solace of silence and comfort I often derived from my meditation group, led by Buddhist teacher Jack Kornfield. Arriving early to our "sitting," I noticed that Jack was early too, readying himself for the evening's class. I approached him hoping for some soothing salve of wisdom.

"Who left who?" he asked when I told him what had happened.

"He left me," I choked. The words still hurt.

"Ah, the bum. Maybe we should send him some poison."

I chuckled. His levity momentarily reconnected me with my wiser self, whom Jack calls "the one who knows."

"Jack, I tell myself there is perfection in the way things are, but I can't seem to stop these murky, heavy clouds from overtaking me when I least expect it. And it's taking so long. We ended it months ago."

He looked at me out of the corner of his eye. "You're grieving. It comes in waves. Then maybe after a little revenge."

I managed a smile as I replied, "I guess I need more patience. Truth be told, these feelings are really familiar. They tell me, 'You're not good enough. You're rejected. You're alone.' I've had them lots of times before. It's almost like they aren't about the breakup at all. I'm hoping this time I can heal the source of this wound."

As I spoke I realized that, although I was sad to say good-bye, it wasn't the relationship ending that hurt so much. It was the *stories* about myself that were causing the real pain: I'll never be able to love someone as much as I loved him. I'm too old or unlovable to meet someone as good as him. Et cetera. These stories were the source of my suffering. The biggest "pinches" in my life had always been triggered by feeling spurned, rejected, abandoned, or ignored.

Before I saw the theme, it was such an issue that an unreturned call, a delayed invitation, or even a tone of voice could send me into a downward spiral. Decades of coaching others have shown me that we each have a particular theme. What we have in common is that most emotional "pinches" are some version of the feeling of being "out," not "in," caused by a deficiency story that is always a derivative of our original core wound—the illusion of separation from source. But knowing that doesn't necessarily bring any relief in the middle of an ow moment.

As we talked, Jack reminded me that, in order to free myself from the habitual pattern of feeling unloved, I needed to seek out and compassionately *be with* the underlying, familiar *feeling* theme of my recurring story. Resisting my dark feelings, fearing they would overwhelm me, wasn't the way through. My wounded feelings needed to be held with love and compassion. It helped to remember that these "not enough" feelings were part of being human.

Looking Ahead

Working with the Co-Creative Power of Feelings in this chapter, you will learn to manage and understand your emotions so that you can feel more balanced and joyful on a daily basis. By trusting in and opening to the awes and ows of life, you will:

- Become more curious and courageous in investigating your feelings
- Claim more emotional freedom by moving more skillfully through uncomfortable feelings
- Free yourself from emotional "pinches" and constricting thought habits
- Learn to generate "feel-good" feelings at will

If your everyday practice is to open to all your emotions, to all the people you meet, to all the situations you encounter, without closing down...you will understand all the teachings that anyone has ever taught.

—Pema Chödrön

Stories

It is natural to want to suppress painful emotions. But when we suppress them we end up acting them out in ways that cause even more pain. As these stories show, what we don't transmute we transmit. Investigating painful emotions doesn't send us down the spiral as we fear, but reveals the pathway from ow to awe.

Susan's Story: Finding Your Path Through the Shadows

At the age of forty-eight, Susan re-authored her life. It began one Sunday when a colleague called to say that Susan's CEO and good friend, Peter, had suffered a fatal heart attack. Susan hung up the phone and stood staring out the kitchen window. The cliché "life is short" suddenly became an intimate reality. Right then and there, Susan decided to leave corporate America to find her calling.

A few nights later she had a dream in which a former therapist counseled her to go meet a woman who would help her in her quest. Susan called the therapist the following day, hoping for some advice on next steps. "The only person who comes to mind is a Buddhist monk in Santa Fe, Roshi Joan Halifax, who leads workshops on death and dying," the therapist told Susan. It wasn't what Susan wanted to hear. Her sister had died ten years before and her stored-up grief had been held down like a beach ball underwater. Peter's recent death forced it to the surface. Yet somehow she knew this trip was the right next step to take.

Susan sat facing a wall with twenty other people. What was she doing in New Mexico at a Zen Buddhist retreat with twenty Buddhists all sitting on hard zafu pillows? Susan had never sat in meditation for more than five minutes. Here, they sat for hours. She made sure to always sit on the zafu closest to the door in case she had to bolt. As discreetly as possible, so as not to distract her neighbor, she jiggled her legs every so often to keep them from falling asleep.

The routine was to rise at 4:30 a.m., sit in meditation for an hour, eat breakfast, and then sit for two more hours. There was lots of bowing and rituals and ringing of bells. Her evenings were often spent attending lectures or reading, but it was the afternoons, when everyone took part in some form of selfless service, that she enjoyed the most. Susan liked kitchen duty, because over the cutting of carrots and the opening of spring peas some of the most meaningful conversations took place. Susan wasn't just a listener anymore, as she was all too frequently in her position as VP of Human Resources. Now, for the first time in a long time, she was also truly being heard.

She told stories of growing up with her sister and what she cherished about her. Her tears seemed to wash away a gray film, revealing a joyfulness like bright sunshine after a dark rain. By the end of her ten-day retreat, her zafu pillow seemed softer, and something in Susan began to open and soften too.

We in the Western world are not customarily comfortable with death. It is viewed as something scary and unspeakable, something kept private in the shadows of our families. Susan recognized that her feelings of fear and avoidance around her sister's death had come from this unconscious cultural imprint. Following the retreat, her compassion for people in the last stage of life grew, and she made a commitment to herself to find a way to help people in both their living and dying. It was the first step on a new, authentic path.

Every morning we must love what is lost in us and begin again.

—Beth Ferris

Stacie's Story: Learning to Live from Love

Stacie found herself frustrated with the man in her life. They had met a year earlier when he was separating from his wife, and Stacie had hoped that they would have moved further along by now. There was no question that she and Ned were in love. They had talked about buying a home together and having kids, and they spent all their free time in each other's company. But after a year, Ned was still not through with his divorce.

By the time we spoke, Stacie's frustration had turned into anger. She wanted to be number one in Ned's life, but instead felt like she was riding shotgun. She had a burning desire to have a baby and feared that she would be past her prime childbearing years by the time Ned was fully extricated and ready to start a new family.

Stacie's voice began to take on an edge whenever she broached the subject with him of moving the relationship forward. Ned, in turn, began to seem less enthusiastic. No one responds well to pressure, and Stacie's anger and "ticking clock" agenda were causing Ned to resist and pull away. It was crucial that Stacie examine her part in this dilemma.

As we talked, Stacie uncovered some similar—but older and buried—feelings about her father. She had often felt ignored and insignificant in the eyes of her alcoholic dad, but never communicated or worked through her hurt and resentment. If we don't process our pain, we will project it. Stacie's stuck feelings were about to derail her life's dream: to have a family with the man she loved.

Our subconscious, made up of unexamined feelings, assumptions, and beliefs downloaded in the past, controls 80 percent of our decisions and actions. If these go unquestioned, like recordings they play out directly in our lives.

Each time we observe and investigate a patterned response, we create space between the trigger and our knee-jerk reaction. We don't need to recall the whole originating scenario; just the act of compassionately witnessing our automatic thoughts and feelings creates more freedom. We become empowered to respond rather than react. We make more intelligent choices.

With her newfound awareness of her very similar feelings about the two men in her life, Stacie could step back and own the source of her anger instead of projecting it onto Ned. With her feelings now close to the surface, she agreed to write a letter to her dad (which she would not send) expressing the anger and hurt that she had held in for so long. Her pen moved fast and furiously until her anger dissolved into tears. Once her sobs subsided, she felt a sense of peace and detachment. Stacie had purged stored-up emotional pain.

Later, she was able to share her experience with Ned, as well as her new understanding of herself and her needs, from a much softer, more vulnerable place. He responded with empathy and love, and trust was restored between them. Within two weeks he had signed papers with his wife, and Stacie and Ned were making plans for their wedding.

Three months later, Stacie's father was diagnosed with cancer. For the first time in her adult life, Stacie could authentically express unreserved love for her dad. No longer identified with her emotional wound, she didn't feel the need to "get" anything from him and so was content just to give. On her visits, she could feel how much he appreciated her presence. "There is no need to even talk. He just enjoys being with me."

Stacie didn't back down on what she wanted with Ned, but she approached it differently by pausing and investigating her feelings with loving curiosity. Equally important, she was able to make peace with her father at a critical time. Ultimately, she learned how to dissolve the barriers to live from love.

The best way out is always through.

—Robert Frost

Exercises

Remember our emotions are not the truth but often the doorway to the truth. Trusting in the awes and ows of our lives means being guided by our hearts rather than our heads in order to find our deeper truth. Working with the exercises here will help you work though difficult feelings to find more peace.

Feeling In and Focusing Up

Life is full of unexpected twists and turns, and we can only exert so much control over the outside world. However, we always have the choice to *learn from* and *manage* our emotions. We learn from our feelings when we think of them as an essential part of our guidance system, supporting us in living true to our potential. A difficult feeling may be informing us that we've gone against our soul's integrity, either by not meeting an important need or by thinking or doing something that contradicts our highest good. On the Spiral journey, these "pinches" are also sacred invitations to heal old emotional wounds and inhabit more of our wholeness.

The next time you feel troubled, excavate your "pinch" for limiting thoughts or unfelt feelings that, once seen and felt, can be released. Use the process that follows to liberate you whenever you find yourself stuck in an emotional downward spiral. You will find that engaging in this inquiry, even a handful of times, will lessen the likelihood of the same "pinch" upsetting you in the future and provide you with a tool to Spiral Up! no matter what happens.

Feeling In and Focusing Up Process

1. What happened that upset you? (Just give the facts, not the feelings.) Examples: my car wouldn't start, my partner and I broke up, an old friend didn't return my call, etc.

2. What did you feel, emotionally and physically, when this happened? Take an inner inventory and come up with at least one example: my stomach felt knotted, I was angry, I started shaking inside.

3. What story are you telling yourself? Take the time to think about and write down what interpretation you're giving to this event, no matter how true, false, or foolish it may seem. Examples: I am not a good mother, my boss thinks I am incapable, I am invisible.

4. Beneath your feelings, is there a deeper feeling? What is it? Under anger might be sadness, under rage might be love, under jealousy might be fear. To identify the deeper, rawer level, try to temporarily suspend whatever interpretation you have attributed to what happened and *feel into* your body for a deeper feeling. Examples: sadness, fear, grief.

5. What is your underlying unmet need? Examples: affection, security, connection.

6. Is there a way that you can provide some element of that for yourself right now? For example, if your need is love, you could call a close friend who is good at providing empathy, or if you need security, you could take some time to assess your financial situation.

7. From your wisest "knowingness," what is a more empowering interpretation of this pinch? Examples: I care deeply about others, I am resilient, there are better fits for my skills and talents.

8. Is there a request that you need to make in order to take care of yourself now or in a similar situation in the future? For example, I need to: ask my husband to share the household tasks, make a request of my boss to be considered for promotion, ask myself to communicate more directly and honestly.

Bless the sacred source of the pinch. Challenges help us to evolve and ascend to our greater selves.

Think higher and feel deeper.

—**Elie Wiesel**

Dramatize It

Remember, "e-motions" are energy that needs to move! When we hold in tears and anger we also hold in joy, creativity, and wisdom. When you cry you get more brilliant. When you laugh you get more imaginative. Loosen and free your feelings by expressing them fully. The next time you feel stuck in an uncomfortable emotion, try one of these techniques:

- Magnify and dramatize whatever emotion you are feeling: growl, sob, howl. Expletives, chest thumping, and wailing are all allowed!
- Shake it! Turn the volume up on music that makes you move. Dance wildly.
- Rock yourself like a baby. Sit on the floor or sofa, wrap your arms around your knees, and soothe yourself by rocking gently back and forth.
- Sing it! Put on your favorite song and sing your heart out.

CAUTION! Do not try this at work.

> If you want to shrink something you must first allow it to expand.
> —*Tao Te Ching*

Highlights

- Susan's story shows us that renewal is possible if we move bravely toward fear.
- Owning and "feeling into" emotional pain can free you from it.
- Completing old feelings creates an opening for good to flow.
- Grieving has its own timeline; it needs our patience and self-compassion.
- Free yourself from "pinches" by questioning your thoughts and responding to your emotional needs.

> Hurt feelings or discomfort of any kind cannot be caused by another person. No one outside me can hurt me. That's not a possibility.
> —Byron Katie

CHAPTER 11

Free Your Voice to
Live Out Loud

The Co-Creative Power of Speech

When every woman learns to listen without fear to the voice inside her instead of smothering it, it may lead— perhaps even more surely than rockets into space—to the next step in human evolution.

—Betty Friedan

Congratulations! You've graduated to the next level of the Co-Creative Power of Speech. Here's where you'll learn to put your voice into the world in a way that serves your higher purpose and the greater good. Ready to turn up the volume on your truth-telling skills?

As women, we are stepping into power positions across our business, educational, political, and cultural landscapes. Gloria Steinem recently acknowledged, however, "In terms of real power—economic and political—we are still just beginning." Until we become aware of how we suppress our true voice and then work at truly liberating it, we are in danger of sabotaging our successes. To expand into our fullest potential, we must learn to speak authentically, in every area of our lives. Living out loud, however, isn't something that we women have been taught to do.

The Roots of our Reticence

Historically, the patriarchal message to women has been to sit down and shut up. In a backlash to that, the feminist movement urged us to stand up and shout (which is equally alienating). Why the need for either message? Girls are often socialized to please others, neutralize conflict, and get along. This need to please hinders our ability to speak assertively and disagree constructively, essential skills in getting our needs met and participating as equals in society.

Eve Ensler, a powerful advocate for women's voices around the world, has traveled to more than sixty countries, studying and working with thousands of girls and women. In her opening remarks at a women's conference, she said, "I've seen over and over, how they [girls and women] have been silenced, muted, crippled, undone, and robbed of authenticity by the enforced and the internalized need to please. *To please is to be the wish or will of somebody other than yourself.*"

In many parts of the world, especially the United States, we have made great strides in women's rights. But even in the U.S. women have been permitted to vote for less than a century. The roots of our reticence run deep. Somewhere in each of us, we carry cellular memory of being punished for being different or outspoken—cast out or even burned at the stake. Silencing ourselves made sense then, in fact it was a smart survival strategy. But today, at least in the free world, finding our voices and using them is life-critical.

Sandy, a straight-talking senior executive, told me of her CEO's dismay at an assertion she made in a board meeting. She said, "Every day you get signals to not be yourself or say certain things. Do we acquiesce and stand down? Become victimized or doused? A lot of us know what needs to be done but we don't think we're smart enough or good enough to speak up and stand up for what we know. We undermine ourselves rather than take the risk of being out of favor."

Even some of our most powerful and accomplished women struggle to find their authentic voices. Jane Fonda reveals in her autobiography, *My Life So Far*, that while incredibly brave and outspoken in her professional, political, and social life, she was disloyal to herself in private. Like many women, she would do anything for the approval and love of others. In Fonda's case, she betrayed herself by not having a voice in her intimate relationships. She admits that she spent much of her time trying to be perfect—not just for men, but to meet some self-imposed, impossible standard. She wrote, "God forbid I should own who I am. It's true of many women—there's this bifurcation between the public and internal, private realities. Becoming whole means bringing those two things together—no matter what."

Fonda counsels us that trying to be perfect is toxic. In fact, she discovered that the true meaning of the word *perfect* isn't "flawless," but comes from the Aramaic for "wholeness." We cannot move toward wholeness, however, until we learn to overcome our fears and speak up for ourselves.

> **The act of pleasing makes everything murky. We lose track of ourselves, we stop uttering declaratory sentences, we stop directing our lives, we wait to be rescued, we forget what we know. We make everything okay rather than real.**
>
> **—Eve Ensler**

The Art of Authenticity

Do you have trouble asking for what you want with certain people? Do you hold back for fear of losing face or even the relationship? Does your mouth sometimes speak before your mind weighs in? Do you speak in ways that dominate, for fear of not being in control? In speaking authentically, where is your "growing edge"?

There is an art to speaking our truth without becoming soulless or harsh. It is possible to speak up in all areas of life—our work, our relationships, our family, with people in public—in ways that honor our needs as well as our relationships. Being able to express our wants and don't-wants is essential. Jennifer Openshaw's book *The Millionaire Zone* cites research showing that the distinguishing factor between people of average means and those with seven figure incomes is the ability that the latter have to access their "life net," or social network, to ask for introductions or support.

Making powerful requests is not only essential to our effectiveness in the world, it's one way we practice living out loud. Other ways include learning to say no, speaking from a place of inner guidance, and breaking through silence to voice the unvarnished truth.

Living out loud doesn't mean speaking brashly or carelessly. The Co-Creative Power of Speech is the skill of communicating consciously with both honesty and kindness. Authentic speaking draws on our feminine ability to *contain* and *incubate* our thoughts, as opposed to the tendency we sometimes have to chatter to fill the silence, blurt something out, or "get it off our chest." When we pause long enough to let our words drop beneath our chests and into our hearts, they convert into truth.

There's a process to learning to speak authentically. We check in with ourselves—"What's the truth for me?" Next we practice articulating our inner experience. Finally, we refine as we go, knowing that as we speak, it becomes clearer to us what we need to say. The point here isn't to get our point across or get what we want, but to see, feel, and express ourselves so that we stay connected to our authentic power.

Anytime we've forgotten who we are, just by speaking our truth, voilà! We remember. How do we find our authentic voice? By sharing our inner experience without an agenda; by saying yes to what ignites us and no to what drains us, and asking for what we need and want in a timely manner.

As we become skillful with the Co-Creative Power of Speech, we speak less carelessly. We drop the hidden meanings or agendas in our messaging. We don't try to prove anything, "get" anything, or manipulate an outcome. We purely relate. We live our lives out loud in ways that honor not only our values but also our wisdom.

Each time we express who we are with our authentic voice, we lay claim to more of ourselves. The Co-Creative Power of Speech requires us to stand in our inherent value and prioritize both our self-expression *and* our connection with others. This act of communicating from a clean, undefended place is both disarming and unifying. It is also only possible when we're connected to our higher self.

Connecting our words to a higher guidance is a sacred, age-old practice. In Native American circles and Quaker meetings, individuals sit in silence to hone and develop their relationship to that higher impulse. They don't utter a word until they feel not just the mind, but the inward stirring of their heart moving them to speak.

As Americans, we're so into "telling it like it is" or saying whatever pops into our minds that we sometimes lose the value of discretion. Not every thought needs to be communicated. When we're connected to our true self we don't speak in order to fill the silence, to get love or approval, or to be right. Speaking authentically leaves no residue, nor does it require second-guessing. It's wonderfully liberating.

Looking Ahead

As you work with the Co-Creative Power of Speech in this chapter, you will identify where you most often lose your authentic voice, and you'll learn how to find it and use it!

As you free your voice to live out loud, you will:

- Swap the "need to please" for communicating your truth
- Speak up in ways that profit you emotionally and financially
- Make powerful requests and declines
- Articulate in ways that create deep connection

> **Women who say what they want—generally successful, high-achieving people—are considered difficult. Divas. Witches. Sluts.**
>
> **—Ellen Tien**

Stories

How often do we get caught in a trap, saying something that we don't really mean or not asking for what we want? And what would it be like to break with that cycle? The stories that follow reveal how sometimes the most powerful thing we can do is make a request, while other times the most powerful form of expression is silence.

Alexis's Story: The Art of Authenticity

Alexis called to speak with me about a problem she was having with Audrey, a more senior colleague whom she had invited to collaborate on a consulting project. Alexis, a big-hearted and gregarious brunette, was troubled because Audrey was "not much of a team player." Sharp and efficient, Audrey had run her own business for decades and was used to working solo.

On their three-way conference calls with clients, instead of positioning herself and Alexis as a team, Audrey would often say things like "I do such and such this way," "This is how I work," and "I'll follow up with you next week on that." Yes, Alexis had brought Audrey in because of her experience, but she thought Audrey should represent them as a team, using the word *we*. Alexis was not shy, but Audrey's dominant style caused her to fade into the background.

As Alexis told me of her predicament, I noticed she was having trouble forming her words. She explained that she had seriously bitten her tongue the day before, causing it to swell. "Hmm," I thought, "this metaphor is painfully obvious!" When I asked her if she felt she needed censoring, she laughed out loud. She realized that even though she wanted to clear the air, there was a more powerful unconscious message telling her, "Bite your tongue!"

When fearful, we edit and hold back, or we become strident and bossy. We speak as if disembodied, a puppet to what we imagine others want to hear or what we think will garner us more power and safety. If we pay attention, our instant feedback system tells us when we're off. This is how the Co-Creative Powers of Feelings and Speech work so beautifully together—they instantaneously inform us. Negativity, manipulation, dishonesty, or speaking to try to impress makes us feel tainted.

Just like Alexis, if we notice that we're about to bite our tongue, we then have a choice. We can let ourselves be seen or we can hide, withhold, or downplay our feelings ("I'm fine!"). When we rationalize with excuses like "I don't want to hurt her feelings" or "I don't want to rock the boat," we're actually sacrificing connection for the illusion of control. By squelching our feelings in favor of *managing* the situation, we forgo the opportunity to "know and be known" at a deeper level.

Alexis could have written Audrey off as "not a team player," or judged herself as less capable and resentfully pulled out of the assignment. But she was committed to their partnership and to showing up authentically; she just needed to find the right words. As we role-played, she practiced communicating in a way that enabled her to truthfully express and release her emotions without getting stuck in them. In her next conversation with Audrey, she said, "I so value your partnership on this project and I'd like to feel that I'm providing as much value as you on our conference calls. Do you have ideas that would help us show up more as a team? I'd love it if, when you mention what we'll provide, you speak of us as 'we' rather than 'I.' "

For a moment the silence was almost deafening. Then Audrey sighed and said, "I'm sorry—I do that! I'm so used to working by myself. I want you to know I really value our collaboration." Audrey promised to represent them as a team going forward and she kept to that promise.

Taking personal responsibility for our experience frees us to speak our truth with genuine confidence and ease. We are neither aggressive toward others, nor do we need to bite our own tongues. We communicate in ways that are transparent, nonjudgmental, and clear.

Jill's Story: Listening for Our Higher Impulse

Standing in her sun-filled kitchen, Jill listened intently to Jacquie's dilemma. Jacquie had met someone new and needed to move out of her former boyfriend's house, but her recent layoff made her financial situation unstable. Without even thinking, Jill offered, "You can move in here."

As soon as her words spilled out, she felt the "clunk" in her energy. She hadn't been feeling particularly generous. In fact, she was tiring of their conversation. She had simply spoken from a conditioned pattern to take care of and please others.

When Jill was a young girl, her widowed mother had relied heavily on Jill's attention and resourcefulness. Jill had figured out: if I pay attention to you, then you'll pay attention to me. Pleasing her mom and being "nice" had become a survival strategy to get love and feel safe. But now it was an identity that felt limiting and oppressive. By jumping in to rescue Jacquie, she exerted control over the situation, but at the cost of her own integrity and needs.

By automatically giving without checking in with ourselves, we reinforce the belief that our needs are less important and we end up resenting the other person. A more authentic move for Jill might have been simply listening and acknowledging the uncertainty of Jacquie's dilemma, even if Jacquie seemed to be asking for a solution. She also had another choice: if she really wanted to, she could offer to help Jacquie come up with a plan of her own.

To be both honest and kind (to ourselves as well as others), we listen for our higher impulse. We go beyond our conditioned response and serve the higher good in the moment. By staying curious and open, and remaining in touch with ourselves moment to moment, we're more mindful of our thoughts and emotions. As we restrain from reacting, our capacity to respond wisely and genuinely deepens.

> **Relating is motivated by the wish to know and be known, to open yourself to another so they can see and perhaps empathize with your experience. Controlling comes from the need to be comfortable and safe, to avoid feeling awkward, uncomfortable, or unsafe.**
> **—Susan Campbell, PhD**

Exercises

Has anyone ever said to you, in a moment of irritation or illumination, "Just listen to yourself"? We don't always grasp what our words are really saying. Or that we're speaking from fear. The exercises that follow will show you how to express yourself with integrity, clarity, and confidence.

Break Your Silence

Anytime we feel afraid to speak our truth, it's because we're caught in the grip of a limiting belief. Once you're aware of the belief, you have already begun to free yourself from its clutches.

What do you tell yourself that stops you from speaking authentically? Examples: I'll make others uncomfortable, people will think that I'm conceited, it's probably a dumb idea.

Consider that your beliefs are often just fear talking. Don't let your fears stop you from living out loud.

> **A voice can get a party started, shout down opponents, or lead a country. Vocal cords are like any other part of your body. They are there to be worked.**
> **—Anna Deavere Smith**

Free Your Voice: Authentic Speaking Quiz

We all have areas where we are susceptible to falling out of integrity with our words. The following exercise will help you discover your growing edge and what you need to do differently in order to speak with more power and authenticity.

On a scale of 1 to 5 (1 being "not at all" and 5 being "frequently"), how much does each statement apply to you?

If others gossip or speak negatively, I join in.
I agree with or flatter people to get them to like me.
I have trouble saying things that I think might hurt others' feelings.
I have difficulty expressing tenderness and vulnerability.
If someone criticizes me, I quickly defend myself.
I find it hard to express jealousy, anger, and hurt.
I have trouble taking credit for something I accomplished.
I shrink from giving others "negative" feedback, even when it's constructive.
I agree to do things that I don't really want to do.
I can speak up for my team and/or my kids more easily than for myself.
I have difficulty asking for what I want with certain people at work.
I feel inhibited asking for what I want in my intimate relationships.

If you scored mostly 4s and 5s, you sometimes sacrifice your authenticity in order to feel safe and comfortable. Please don't beat yourself up for it! We all do it from time to time. Just becoming aware of when and how you do it will begin the process of changing it.

> **It took me quite a long time to develop a voice, and now that I have it, I am not going to be silent.**
> **—Madeleine Albright**

Authentic Speaking Goals

Now that you've zeroed in on some trouble spots, think about how you'd like to communicate instead. Select your top three communication challenges from the Authentic Speaking Quiz, then turn each one around to set a goal for new ways of relating to others that are truer to yourself. Examples: I will refrain from gossip, I will not be defensive, I will take credit for my accomplishments.

Think about your Authentic Speaking Goals, write them in your journal, and imagine yourself responding in a new, authentic manner in each scenario.

> **Truth is always exciting. Speak it, then. Life is dull without it.**
>
> —Pearl S. Buck

Making Powerful Requests

From the personal to high-stakes business situations like asking for a raise, shrinking yourself so as to not look too aggressive is costly. Another reason women hold themselves back is to be modest, but modesty is not authentic, it is an attempt to not come off as arrogant. When we are genuinely in touch with our greatness (or even the greatness of another) it evokes humility—we feel humbled.

And it has been estimated that women pay a steep financial price for modesty—over the course of a career, not negotiating salary increases has been estimated to cost a million dollars or more. But making powerful requests isn't just about money.

Making powerful requests requires that we step beyond our comfort zone to express a need or want. In turn, it should give the "requestee" an opportunity to stretch beyond her norm as well. A powerful request includes specifics about what you want as well as what it will mean to you or others when it is fulfilled (the "why"). It also incorporates details like "by when" and "by whom" and is stated in such a way that it elicits a response. Here are the essential elements as laid out by Fernando Flores, leader in the world of business process design:

- Requester: Who is asking?
- Requestee: Who is being asked?

- Future action: What do I want you to do (and a little bit of why)?
- Conditions of satisfaction: How will I know it's been done? (i.e., a measurable outcome)
- Time: By when?

Many of us, especially women, tend to use forms of request that are less effective because they're passive, vague, or hesitant, or because they leave out some of those key details.

Common less-effective forms of request:

- Would you mind ... ?
- Why don't you ... ?
- _____ needs to be done.
- Can you ... ?

Powerful requests often take one of these forms:

- I ask that you ...
- I request ...
- Will you please _____ by _____?

When you ask for what you want, paint a picture for the other person, giving as much detail as you can about what you want and what vision this serves.

—Susan Campbell, PhD

Just Say No

Bonnie, the receptionist at my dentist's office, asked if I'd like to attend the fund-raiser for the local school. My "no" was met with a huge "Thank you!" She explained, "I hate it when people say, 'Let me check my schedule,' as if their calendar is their decision maker. They already know the answer but are afraid to say no."

If asking for what we want is one side of a coin, the flip side is declining what we don't. More than 80 percent of us have trouble saying no, according to a survey by Mary M. Byers, author of *How to Say No...and Live to Tell About It: A Woman's Guide to Guilt-Free Decisions.* Sometimes no is the right answer. This is particularly the case when by saying no, we're really saying yes to something else. What would life be like if we said no to what we think "they" want and instead said yes to what really calls to us? How would it be different if we tuned out the "shoulds" on behalf of what inspires and moves us?

I am not proposing we shirk our responsibilities and obligations; I'm merely suggesting that we check for any self-imposed, life-draining fates. When year after year we automatically show up for a job that no longer fits or a relationship that no longer feeds us, it exacts a huge toll. When we automatically say yes to the endless stream of minor requests, they nibble away at our life force, leaving us less available for what is really ours to do. Bottom line: until you have a strong no, you'll always have a weak yes.

If your mouth keeps saying yes when you really mean no, ask yourself where the disconnect is:

Are you afraid of missing out on something?
Do you think that if you say no, people won't like you?
Do you tell yourself that if you don't do it, it will never get done?
Are you concerned that others will think you're not a team player?

Consider the possibility that the opposite is true. Receiving and making lots of "stretch" requests and offers is one of the hallmarks of a leader. Powerful people get lots of requests and must frequently say no.

What do you need to say no to? Examples: the numerous calls from my mom/partner/friend, organizing office birthday parties, chairing a committee.

Whom do you need to say no to? Examples: partner, boss, sister.

I've learned that you shouldn't go through life with a catcher's mitt on both hands; you need to be able to throw some things back.

—Maya Angelou

"Just Say No" Tips:

> Thanks, but I have too many other things on my plate right now.
>
> That won't work for me today; however, I can send someone to help you with that. How would that work for you?
>
> I appreciate your invitation, but I'm not planning anything extracurricular right now.
>
> I know how important this is, but I'm not in a position to say yes.
>
> Thank you for asking me, but I cannot do that.
>
> No, thanks, I don't want to do that.
>
> It is not going to work for me to do that.
>
> Thanks, but I don't care to.
>
> Thanks for asking, but I can't commit to that right now.
>
> Unfortunately, that won't work. Let me offer this alternative commitment.
>
> I can't take that on.
>
> You can count on that action by [time], but not right now.
>
> Thanks, but my plate is full.

Saying no doesn't have to mean a flat refusal. There are ways to skillfully decline what doesn't serve you. First of all, humor lubricates! Try saying this with a smile on your face and in your voice: "I appreciate your confidence in me, but I'm actually not Superwoman! Let me tell you when I *can* get that done."

And remember to be authentic. Lying—even if it's what we call a white lie—leaves a residue.

Trust the wisdom of no. If it is the truth, something magical will happen.

—Dr. Robin L. Smith

Truth-Telling: When to Contain and Refrain

Being authentic doesn't have to mean saying things that hurt others. If the truth is cruel, it's not the truth. Our truth bubbles up from a deeper place than our opinions, judgments, and criticisms. It's never about being right; it's about expressing what we think and feel in an authentic, transparent, and undefended way. If our intention is to connect with another, we find ways of communicating our "truth" so that it can be received.

Speaking from the heart means dropping into our feelings and desires and then choosing what to say or not say. Sometimes speaking up is what's called for, and other times it's more powerful to show some restraint. Either way, when we check in first with our intention, it's more efficient. We don't have to go back and clean up any messes we made.

How do you know when to refrain and contain? If you feel an urgent need to say something, it's often a clue that you are reacting to an emotional pinch. It's a good rule of thumb never to communicate when upset. Try waiting an hour, a day, even a week, and notice the metamorphosis of your message. This applies to e-mails, too!

Before speaking (or sending communications), ask yourself, "Why am I sharing this?" If it is it to look good, to be liked, or to make someone else wrong, contain yourself.

You will learn a lot about yourself this way. Take responsibility for the feelings evoked in you. Afterward, there may still be a message to send, but it will be coming from your intention to create connection and understanding, not to control.

Highlights

- A "need to please" can sabotage your ability to speak up and stand up for what you know.
- The Co-Creative Power of Speech is the skill of communicating with both honesty and kindness.
- Authentic speaking is sharing your inner experience without an agenda.
- We "relate" when we self-disclose; we "control" when we speak inauthentically in order to feel safe.
- Making powerful requests and declines is a hallmark of a strong leader.

CHAPTER 12

Harness the Grace of Wise Effort

The Co-Creative Power of Action

You are here to enable the divine *purpose* of the universe to unfold. That is how important you are.
—Eckhart Tolle

There's a wonderful story about two warring tribes in the Andes, the lowlanders and the mountain people. One day the mountain people invaded the lowlanders, abducting a baby and taking her back up into the high mountains. Discovering the child was missing, the enraged lowlanders formed a search party of their strongest warriors to climb the steep and arduous trails to retrieve her.

After half a day of inching forward and sliding backward, the lowlanders had traveled only a short distance up the thickly forested mountain. The men tried first one method of climbing and then another, but after several days they had ascended only a few hundred feet, their novice climbing skills no match for the precipitous slopes. Exhausted and defeated, they were packing up their gear when they noticed a woman making her way down from the highest reaches of the mountain. They realized it was the mother of the kidnapped baby. The baby was strapped to her back.

One man greeted her and exclaimed, "We couldn't climb this mountain. How did you do this when we, the strongest and most able men in the village, couldn't do it?"

She shrugged her shoulders and said, "It wasn't your baby."

Our Souls' Assignments

As this story by author Jim Stovall reminds us, we instinctively know what is ours to do. When we act on it, it can unlock extraordinary reserves of energy. When we find something we are passionate about, something that draws out our talents and gifts in service to what we care about, we tap into a rare strength, exuberance, and joy. *We can also chose to bring that kind of full engagement to whatever we're doing.*

Each of us has our own "soul assignments," perfectly designed situations that draw out our gifts and help us grow into the ever-expanding chambers of our spiral. Caroline Myss refers to these as our sacred contracts. She says, "You have fundamental agreements that you simply feel. You can't put your finger on them because they reveal themselves to you within the context of your life through coincidence, synchronicity, and obligations you can't get out of."

We each receive the exact measure of difficulty, the ideal built-in problems, the right body, and the perfect relationships to self-ACTualize. These aren't in some far off future land but right in front of us. However, it is up to each of us to enlist in our own awakening. Often we live half-heartedly, as if we're at a dress rehearsal, holding back the best of ourselves for some future time when we imagine it will really count.

In her famous line, Martha Graham eloquently expresses the consequences of this misconception: "There is a vitality, a life force, an energy, a quickening that is translated through you into action, and because there is only one of you in all of time, this expression is unique. And if you block it, it will never exist through any other medium and be lost." When we awaken to our soul promise to live authentically and use our gifts to make a difference, we find heaven on earth, and our existence can be a hell when we do not. Finding our authentic purpose is not some obscure mystery to solve or some treasure hunt outside of ourselves. It is the unleashing of our unique constellation of passions, gifts, and "Buddha nature"—the inherent qualities of compassion, understanding, and wisdom that lie within each of us. It's the opening of our hearts, the quieting of our minds, and the giving of ourselves fully to whatever is ours to do.

Red Lights, Green Lights

Ironically, the times that it seems most difficult to act from our Buddha nature offer the greatest opportunities for our transformation: for instance, when no one is looking, where we don't have to, when no one else is doing it, where we won't get credit for it, when we know our goodwill will not be reciprocated, when we just don't feel like it—or when we are afraid.

Wise effort often means we have to get ourselves to do what doesn't come naturally. Sometimes just thinking about making an audacious move can make our hands sweat or our skin crawl. But fear—the main deterrent that stops us from moving toward our dreams—takes many shapes and forms. Let's look at some of the most common obstacles, or red lights, to wise effort. The more familiar you are with what stops you, the less power these "stop" signals will have over you. And if you are stuck on a certain action to take as you progress toward a higher expression for your life, understanding the following red lights may help get you moving again.

What's Stopping You?

Following are some of the most common red lights that get in the way of making progress, followed by green-light thinking which will get you back in gear. Which ones apply to you?

Red light: I don't know my "true" purpose. Your purpose is not some arcane, needle-in-a-haystack function that you have to figure out. It is all the things you do that light you up and help others. Your purpose is to know yourself as a creator, and to get good at being an intentional one. What that really means is, pay attention to your life right now and learn to follow what has energy for you.

Red light: I can't see the big picture. Author E. L. Doctorow once said, "Writing a novel is like driving a car at night. You can see only as far as your headlights, but you can make the whole trip that way." The same is true for life. All you need is the next "right" step in front of you. Once you take that step, the very next one will be revealed to you. These small, incremental, soul-guided actions are enough to deliver you to your destiny.

Red light: It feels too hard. It's climbing the mountain that teaches us how to climb. The first few steps (or more) won't always feel natural; in fact, they may be downright daunting. That means that as you approach something you really want, if it's challenging, you're doing something right!

Red light: I feel like an imposter. Realize that this is a commonly held fear of many successful people. It's only a problem if you allow it to stop you. Start acting yourself into a new way of thinking rather than trying to think yourself into a new way of acting. This is also known as the Enactment Principle, "Act as if," or "Fake it 'til you make it!"

Red light: I'm waiting until conditions (or I) get better. Will Rogers said, "If you wait until you are ready, you will wait forever." Ask any new mom. She'll tell you that she wasn't prepared, but she learned on the fly. All we need is a little faith in our capacity to rise to whatever challenge presents itself, and a sense of humor when we miss. In improvisational theater, anytime we miss a cue or say something that sounds stupid, we're taught to throw our arms up in the air and yell, "Whoo-hoo!" Try this whenever you blunder. It will remind you that it's not that big a deal in the larger scheme of things.

Red light: I act without reflecting. Have you ever caught yourself pushing, manipulating, or trying to "make" something happen by controlling someone or something? When we're fearful, instead of being empowered we try to over-power. That's when we need to listen inside. Where we find our heart's directions, we will find the faith and courage to proceed in a way that leaves room for the universe to conspire.

Red light: I take two steps forward and one step back. If you can't seem to get into gear on something you keep saying you really want, ask yourself if you have a competing intention. For instance, if you have a desire to get promoted, but you're also committed to not making waves, you'll stay in port forever. Or if you want to lose weight but you have the powerful emotional intention to be comforted (and food is the main way you have discovered to nurture yourself), your diet will fail. Tease apart your competing intentions and choose which one you will champion.

Red light: I reflect without acting. One of my clients once said about procrastination, "You can't steer a parked car." Procrastination, self-doubt, and perfectionism all stem from fear of failure. Be like the toddler who falls down and picks herself right up again. When she topples over, she doesn't give up and think, "Oh, I guess walking wasn't meant to be."

And don't imagine or believe that you have to implement some humongous life change or monumental makeover. If you'll just go ahead and take even a small step on behalf of your heart and soul, fear becomes impotent. Nothing shuts it up faster than proof that you *can* do it. And on the way, you can remind yourself that it isn't just your own ideas or strength you are relying on, it's your divine evolutionary impulse pressing on you to ACTualize.

Every situation and relationship in your life—contentious neighbors, a critical boss, the loss of someone dear, a seemingly insurmountable project, or a plan that keeps on failing—is a soul assignment, perfectly designed to heal old wounds and evoke your gifts. When you fully engage with it, it feels right and good and gives you the opportunity to live life at a higher level. You can also take initiative and be proactive in picking juicy challenges—soul goals—instead of letting the universe pick for you. Consider taking on a project that will demand a new set of skills or a new level of maturity. And remember, the "right" thing to do isn't necessarily the easiest. But when we take the next "right" step, regardless of whether anyone else does, we fulfill our soul assignments and Spiral Up!

> **It's when you reach for something greater than you that you start being lived instead of just living.**
> **—Sofia Diaz**

Looking Ahead

As you work with the Co-Creative Power of Action in this chapter, you will be inspired to move through obstacles that up until now have stopped you from creating the life you desire.

As you practice harnessing the grace of wise effort, you will:

- Gain clarity of purpose and vision
- Become aware of self-sabotaging habits and break them
- Detect important clues to your true gifts and destiny
- Recognize the specific strengths and wisdom that your soul assignments are developing in you
- Unleash your power to act on behalf of what really matters

Stories

"Jump and the net will appear." We've heard that saying a million times, but what does it really mean? The following stories give substance to those words, showing us how when we put one foot in front of the other, in service of our soul's calling, the universe supports us.

Wendy's Story: My Mountain to Climb

David had read up on the Kalalau Trail hike even before we left for our vacation to the island of Kauai. Originally built in the 1800s, it is still the only land access to the famous Na Pali Coast. *Pali* means "cliffs." If I had bothered to read the guidebook, I might have realized that. I might also have reconsidered the "eleven-mile hike traversing towering sea cliffs and lush valleys." But David was really excited about it, and I was up for an adventure.

The trailhead should have tipped me off. The first two hundred feet scaled up at an angle of about seventy degrees—to me it looked vertical. It had been raining a lot and the rocks were covered in slick red mud. But, I reasoned, trails often look difficult at the onset; surely it would flatten out.

It took enormous concentration to navigate each rock without slipping off. I began to feel leg muscles I had long forgotten. A cold wind blew through my jacket, and my forehead was beaded with sweat. I wanted to be a trouper and show David, an avid hiker, how strong and courageous I was. Even more, I wanted to experience this adventure. But after thirty minutes of ever-ascending rocks and deepening mud, a flicker of fear bubbled up from my solar plexus. My mind started to fill with worrisome thoughts: I might fall and hurt myself. What happens if we get there and I don't have the energy to come back? Right then, a rosy-cheeked couple came around a hairpin turn on their way back down the trail with the telltale mud stains down their left sides. I asked, "How was it? Were you able to do the whole hike?"

"No way," they replied. "We were just really happy that we got this far!"

We had reached a higher elevation and the wind began to blow hard. As we made it around the next bend, we were rewarded by breathtaking ocean views. Just then another mud-splattered couple hurried past us on their way down. I yelled to be heard over the howling wind, "Why are you coming down?" "Oh, boy," they said, "it is *really* windy. We didn't want to get blown off the trail."

For the next hour, I scuttled along the jagged edges of the cliffs and of my own anxiety as I mediated the two sides of me. One side of me was terrified: What if...? I can't! The other side was calm and reassuring: One step at a time. You don't need to hurry. You can do it!

It was two hours into the hike when I caught sight of a white-haired hiker striding past us from behind. He must have read the terror in my face, because he looked right into my eyes, grinned, and said, "How is it going?" Dressed in pristine white shorts and shirt and leaning on a professional-looking walking stick, he appeared like the spirit of the mountain. His smiling eyes beamed. I squeaked out, "Have you done this before?" "Oh, yes—this is my third time, and I'll tell you, it doesn't get any easier!" His gaze pierced me, radiating a message: I can do this! You can do this! Something in the brightness of his stare penetrated through my fear to touch the part of me that is unstoppable. In that moment, I took the challenge. If he can do it, so can I. My conviction kicked in. I found that I wanted to climb this mountain, and I believed that I could.

David and I had been grabbing onto tree branches to swing over deep crevasses and running to jump over ever-widening pud-dles. I envied the hikers with walking sticks. "I would be far less anxious if I had a walking stick," I said to David. As I looked up, I couldn't believe my eyes: two uniformed men were working on either side of the path, cutting down saplings with their machetes and stacking them into piles. I was astonished that anyone would climb so many miles up a perilous path to do a job. "Would you please cut us some walking sticks?" I asked excitedly. After a few quick snips, they happily handed them over to us. As I felt the stur-diness of the stick in my hand, I sensed that I was not only seen by the universe but supported by it.

At the start of our climb, when our dreams are embryonic, we're vulnerable to other people's projections and fear. A word of discouragement can make us want to turn back. But the more you engage the Co-Creative Power of Action to step into your poten-tial, the more you are aided by grace and transformed. As the famous mountain climber W. H. Murray wrote, "The moment one definitely commits oneself, then Providence moves too." Somewhere on that mountain, the act of climbing it stretched me to new proportions.

Looking back, I know it would have been fine to turn around at any point. Sometimes the right thing to do is to say, "This path isn't for me; I'm not going any further." But I could sense that I was being challenged by something more treacherous than the slippery rocks and steep cliffs. If I had turned back I would have reinforced those disempowering thoughts and never received the surge of strength and support I felt when I finally committed to my own sense of adventure and challenge. Fear often tries to convince me that I am not capable of doing what I really can do. I delighted in breaking free of its hold.

Linda's Story: In Search of the Feminine

Linda, a successful, fifty-something owner of a string of Super-Cuts salons, planned to one day turn her company over to her hardworking employees. But she didn't have a sense of what she wanted next for herself, except to be in love. This is how she articulated her vision:

> I am married to a kind, sensitive, and loving man. He and I have a nurturing and supportive partnership that contributes not only to each of us but to all the other important relationships in our lives. We both feel we have found our soul mate and are committed to each other for the rest of our lives. We also have a shared vision to contribute to a better world. This has made our relationship strong, deep, and powerful. We both feel so incredibly grateful to have found each other.

In her heart, Linda knew that experiencing a deeply loving partnership was a huge part of her soul's learning. She had proven her masculine prowess by making things happen many times over; now it was time to open to her inner feminine and discover the power of her softer, feeling side.

Searching for answers, Linda took a trip to Ecuador and was entranced by the culture, and by the rainforest and its wildness. She felt she was being dipped in the wild feminine, and she hungered for more. So she signed up for a guided trip that would take her deeper into the rainforest. A few days into the trip, she noticed how attentive, caring, and compassionate the skillful guide was; he embodied the balance of masculine and feminine she was calling forward in herself.

During this guided trip, Linda went to see a shaman (a tribal medicine man) who told her, "You are looking for someone to hold your soul." His words unleashed a torrent of tears and a sorrow buried deep inside her. Recognizing the deep truth of his words made her feel like she was coming home.

Linda decided to extend her stay. She signed up for a Spanish immersion class and arranged to live with a local family while she studied. The first week into her language program, she ran into the rainforest guide she had met six months earlier on their expedition. Over coffee, Daniel confided that he had been going through a difficult loss. They found solace in each other's company, and they grew closer. A year later they were married. Linda had manifested her heart's desire.

Today, Linda and Daniel live in a beautiful home that they built together at the edge of the rainforest. She has her partner, not only in a man she loves, but also in the geographical landscape that draws out her deeply feminine side. Her vision inspired her to go for her deepest desires, but it was her willingness to courageously follow her heart's tugs, not knowing where they would lead her, that enabled her to realize her dreams.

I've watched hundreds of clients make a leap of faith that realigns them with the magic of the universe. Equally valuable are the rewards they receive from the expanded perception of their own power and potential. When we act, we discover the strength that lies within each of us.

The Co-Creative Power of Action is the final power because it reminds us that we have to act ourselves into things—we can't just imagine what we want and then expect it to happen to us. When we take bold moves on our own behalf, we won't know the outcome. Like Linda, we simply follow our inner whispers and take the next step. And sometimes magic happens.

Exercises

What wise effort is yours to do? Let these exercises help you pinpoint ways to tap into the goodness and grace that emerges when you act on behalf of your soul's true purpose.

Living Intentionally: Five-Year Vision

There is a story about a man who, upon learning the life expectancy for the average American, figured out that he had about twenty years left. He treasured his weekends, so he decided to figure out how many weekends remained. He said, "It took me until I was fifty-five years old to think about all this in any detail, and by that time I had lived through twenty-eight hundred Saturdays. I got to thinking that if I lived to be seventy-five, I only had about a thousand of them left to enjoy."

To help himself remember that the time he had left was finite, he purchased a large, clear plastic container and filled it with a thousand marbles. Every weekend, he removed one marble and threw it away, reminding himself how precious time is and that once it is gone, it's gone. As he watched the marbles diminish, he became more and more intentional about focusing on the really important things in life.

Our lifespan is finite, too! Let's live it intentionally.

First, estimate your remaining lifespan. What is the approximate age you think you will live to?

What is your current age?

Subtract your current age from your life expectancy and divide by five. How many five-year increments do you have left?

Acknowledging that our lives are finite isn't morbid—it lights a fire under us to seize the life we have and appreciate all of it. Take a moment right now to connect with the deepest part of yourself. From that vantage point, what do you want to make sure happens no matter what? How will you use your remaining five-year increments?

List a minimum of three experiences, events, or results you must create or have before you die. Examples: enjoy a healthy, loving relationship with my partner, make an impact in others' lives, be peaceful inside, become a mother, make a difference for (cause), travel to _____, write and publish a book.

> **I find the great thing in this world is not so much where we stand, as in what direction we are moving.**
> **—Oliver Wendell Holmes, Sr.**

Red Lights into Green Lights

What stops you in your tracks? Choose one or two red lights from the following list that cause you to come to a screeching halt. Then, for one week, try the corresponding green light practice to get yourself going!

I don't know my "true" purpose.
I can't see the big picture.
I want it to feel right first.
I feel like an imposter.
I'm waiting until conditions (or I) get better.
I act without reflecting.
I have competing intentions (two steps forward, one step back).
I reflect without acting.

I don't know my "true" purpose. Green light practice: Do anything this week that both lights you up and helps others. It doesn't have to be the be-all and end-all "purpose" of your life! For example: volunteer at a soup kitchen, perform one song at the open-mike night at your neighborhood pub, offer one of your true gifts in exchange for someone else's, sign up to plan the next office party, and so on.

I can't see the big picture. Green light practice: Considering the prospect of a new career, your life after divorce, or taking on a project that seems insurmountable—remember, the way you eat an elephant is one bite at a time. What is the next small concrete step you can take toward your new future today?

It feels too hard. Green light practice: Remind yourself that at first, it's normal to feel like you don't know what you're doing. Give yourself permission to make mistakes. Ask a friend to support you in doing the thing that scares you, and acknowledge yourself for marshalling wise effort in the direction of your dreams.

I feel like an imposter. Green light practice: If this is your red light, make a list of at least five accomplishments that prove the fallacy of this fear. Then "playact" as if your visions and images of the future are happening right now. Acting "as if" is self-fulfilling.

I'm waiting until conditions (or I) improve. Green light practice: Take one baby step on behalf of a soul goal each day this week (make a call, do some research, sign up for a webinar, open a savings account). Notice how, by taking action even when you don't feel ready, you improve the "situation." Taking those first small steps can ultimately make a huge difference in our lives.

I act without reflecting. Green light practice: Take a walk and contemplate the "final frame" of your vision. What will it look and feel like when you're there? Now, back into it to determine what you would need to do this week to be on track for what you really want. Start one of the following daily practices: prayer, meditation, or reading something spiritual and uplifting.

I take two steps forward, one step back. Green light practice: Conflicting thoughts and feelings need to be brought to the surface or the one that's more emotionally driven will win out regardless of your true intention. It takes wise effort to bring our hidden intentions to conscious awareness. Check in with both sides of yourself. What wants to? What doesn't? If you like, you can give voice to your dueling intentions in your journal. Negotiate a resolution and choose the one you will honor, or consider a way forward that honors both.

I reflect without acting. Green light practice: Ask yourself, "Why must I do this?" and "What will my life be like in two years if I don't?" When we're in touch with the "why" of our soul goals, we gladly take ownership. Make one micro-movement toward your soul goal every day this week.

There is an inner gravity constantly pulling you into your fit in the world.

—David Whyte

Sandpaper for the Soul

Tibetan Buddhist nun Jetsunma Tenzin Palmo lived in a remote Himalayan cave for twelve years. In a lecture I attended, she relayed her perspective on adversity. "We are like rough wood," she said. "If we stroke ourselves with silk we don't become smooth. We need sandpaper. But we don't have to look for sandpaper; it is everywhere."

Soul assignments can seem like sandpaper grating on the tender parts of our selves. But everything that opposes us is actually inviting us to develop more of the qualities of our spiritual essence. We do that by acting with faith and confidence on behalf of our values and integrity. When we put forth wise effort in the face of fear, we transform.

Have you ever really worried about doing something, and then when you actually did it, it was much less intimidating than you thought? Anytime you overcome a fear to take a risk or confront adversity, you accomplish a soul assignment.

Recall a few soul assignments that weren't as formidable as you once feared. Examples: getting married, speaking in public, starting a business, becoming a mother.

What's one example of how this soul assignment served you? Examples: I am more loving, I have more confidence, I don't sweat the small stuff.

In order to persevere, what strengths or wisdom did you draw upon or develop? Examples: courage, trust, optimism.

What is one soul assignment that you are currently in the midst of? Examples: searching for a new job, engaging in an intimate relationship, dealing with an unappreciative boss.

How could you apply the wisdom or strength you gained from a past soul assignment to your biggest challenge today? Examples: the self-love that you developed out of ending a relationship could help you forgive an old resentment; the confidence you gained in mastering a sport could embolden you in starting a new job.

If your current soul assignment were to persist for another five years, what character strengths or gifts would it develop in you? Examples: personal power, forgiveness, commitment.

In what ways could you demonstrate that quality more in your life right now?

Journal your response now.

The obstacle is the path.

—Zen proverb

Highlights

- You will be rewarded with grace from wise effort because heart-driven actions are divinely supported.
- We realize our purpose by opening our hearts, quieting our minds, and giving ourselves fully to whatever is ours to do.
- "Soul assignments" are relationships and situations that catalyze our growth.
- It's good to be sufficiently challenged, even if at times you feel like you don't know what you're doing.
- The "Imposter Syndrome" may arise if you are boldly stepping into the unknown—just don't give it your power!
- When you act from your commitment to be your divinely inspired self, you access personal power, inspire those around you, and expand your capacity to make a positive impact.
- Nothing shuts fear up faster than actions that show you *can* do it.

The Third Turning

Inspiration

Congratulations! You've completed the First and Second Turnings and are now poised to discover the full force of the Spiral to create your most passionate, spiritually fulfilling, and positively impactful life. What's different about this turning is that, instead of you pursuing your purpose, it will begin to choose you. And you'll know it, because you'll receive invitations to show up in a bigger way. There will still be times when your mind will try to talk you out of it by telling you to play safe. Our fears of being consumed by other people's needs or directives, or simply being overtaken by too many demands, can cause us to hesitate to step up to this next level of expression and evolution. We can equate living larger with soul-crushing sacrifices.

But what if you could play by your own rules? Taking on that next level of leadership will likely require more of you than before, so what would you need to put in place in order to stay connected to yourself? Who could be your "board of directors" to keep you positive, energized, and pointed in the right direction? And would it be worth it to fall out of balance now and then in order to play at a new level of contribution and impact? Remember, safety and comfort are not the priorities when you are called to live a wholehearted life.

In this Third Turning, you will feel the arrival of a newfound freedom to love, play, and give freely of the very best of you. Love is the core of who you are. It is not something that you generate as much as something that you allow. Your desire to evolve, to create, and to serve others is an expression of that love. Grace enters your life as you choose moment to moment to live true to your heart. It's not that you're perfect, or that your life is working out just as you planned, but that you feel inspired because you are participating in something bigger than yourself: you sense a divine direction for your life.

These are times to invite that rollicking, unstoppable energy of your true self to rip. In a world that often seeks to reduce everything down to being liked and getting ahead, being riveted by life—playing full out—is truly a courageous and glorious way to live. Only by connecting with and contributing to the world around us, and what we care about, do we discover a deeper level of interdependence, interconnectedness, and fulfillment. We are buoyed by like-minded souls and a delicious sense of belonging. We are actively living our part in the greater story.

So let me ask you: Are you ready to enter the third tier of the Spiral? Are you ready to become the co-creator of your life?

CHAPTER 13

Unleash the Power of Your Passion

The Co-Creative Power of Energy

Passion is authentic power.

—**Gary Zukav**

A few years back, I attended a party brimming with creative social entrepreneurs, many of them involved in high-tech solutions to positively influence the future. The room buzzed with excitement.

At one point, I wandered outside onto the deck. A throng of people, triple-tier deep, was gathered around a petite, light-haired woman in her forties. I was struck by her radiance, the way she glowed in response to each person with whom she spoke. A quiet, silky energy emanated from her with every word and gesture. I was drawn to her as someone might be drawn to a fire on a cold night. Her vibration—understated, loving, and powerful—was so unlike the scintillating, excited energy of most of the attendees that I was captivated. I didn't know who this woman was, what she did, or what she cared about. I only knew that I felt deeply attracted to her presence. She vibrated at a higher frequency.

Later, after getting to know Claudia, I discovered that she had been developing this deep, loving energy in a systematic way for many years. Her life had not been easy. But instead of being diminished by the challenges, she felt compelled to cultivate a serene energy state regardless of the circumstances. The energy she exuded made other people feel loved and cared for because she was fully loving and caring for herself. I was reaching for the same inner peace and radiance. Today, I know that serene energy is available to me in any moment. And it can be available to you, too.

As you know by now, your energy is an invisible but powerful force through which you receive and transmit information, whether consciously or unconsciously. You've learned to recognize that everything you think, feel, say, or do changes your energy and, hence, the circumstances of your life. You've practiced working with your energy consciously as a tool for inner transformation and to shift to a more open, flowing state.

In the Third Turning, you will dissolve the most persistent barriers to your naturally radiant and powerful presence and learn to deliberately emanate energy that feels confident, good, and engaged with life. Your most authentic self is your evolutionary self: kind, loving, and wholehearted. When you connect to these qualities and begin to cultivate and express them, you inhabit your true self—you tap into your spiritual energy. This passionate, magnetic, and irresistible Co-Creative Power of Energy, in its purest expression, is the energy of love. And it can put you effortlessly into alignment with your highest good.

From Fear into Love

Jerry Jampolsky's pioneering book *Love Is Letting Go of Fear* taught me that the only thing standing between us and the awesome energy of love is fear. Fear is the language of our ego and love is the language of our soul. I'm not referring to romantic love, but the kind of love we experience every day in its many flavors, such as empathy, compassion, appreciation, passion, faith, or simply caring for another. This spiritual energy of love only gets obscured when "pinched" off or "kNOTted" up due to a temporary (or chronic) constriction of heart or mind. You've heard people say, "He's shut down" or "She's very closed-minded." They are referring to the ego's stranglehold on our energy. To participate in the conscious creation of our lives, our energy must be free and flowing.

At times it feels almost impossible to not succumb to anger, depression, or perhaps a sludgy energy that arrives upon waking one morning. But we are in control of our energy. At any time, we can choose to shift from our "biographical" self, our ego, to our deeper identity; from our instinctual "survival" self, which believes we are separate and alone, to our spiritual self that knows we are interconnected and part of an exquisite plan unfolding our greatest good.

The energy we embody swings between these two extremes. If we are controlling, defensive, or attached to an outcome, our energy is fearful and closed. When we are welcoming, compassionate, and trusting in the friendliness of the universe, our loving, radiant, spiritual energy shines through us, opening us to life and possibilities.

A Passion for Life

When our energy is unabashedly flowing, we feel passionate. Passion unlocks the physical and spiritual energy necessary to achieve goals. Think of someone you know who has seemingly unlimited energy—the kind of energy that sparks and uplifts and rouses us to pursue a greater vision. Passionate people teach us how to live from love. They are inspired by life and eagerly pour out their gifts at ever-expanding levels. We are all meant to be an outlet for that immense source that goes by many names: God, universal energy, chi, the divine, creative intelligence, love, or spirit.

When our vessel is clear and spacious, spirit easily and freely expresses through us. The right food, exercise, relationships, creativity, and work all contribute to our energy flowing. But even without those things, spiritual energy is always available to invigorate us. We get "juiced" simply by recognizing that we are each an expression of this divine energy of love.

Whether we are taking care of children, growing a company, writing poetry, developing people, or caring for the sick, when we are in touch with the spiritual energy of love we are in our right place in the world. There is no limit to spirit's ability to demonstrate through our lives, but we must be willing givers and receivers. We all have our own personal renewable energy source that is inexhaustible as long as we honor our need for replenishment. As we summon this energy to meet the challenges and vision we are called to, it becomes the fuel for our focus, determination, and resilience.

Right now, you are being called to emanate your unique version of this divine energy. As you move through the Third Turning of the Spiral you will experience for yourself how to free more of your energy to live as love and joy: not the jumping-up-and-down kind of excitement, but the deep contentedness and overriding feeling of gratitude that resides within.

At the deepest level you are a field of energy connected to the cosmic energy—you should have unlimited energy, creativity, imagination, insight.

—Deepak Chopra

The Power of Presence

Author and teacher David Deida once told me that I would attract my life partner not by something I did or said, but with my energy: "You could be ordering a cappuccino at Starbucks and simply the way you turn and reach for the cup will be so filled with presence and sensuality that your future partner will say, 'I need to meet her.'"

Deida met his own partner that way. At a dinner party, one of the guests dropped his knife. A woman reached down to pick it up to return it to its owner. In that moment, Deida was lovestruck. This woman's energy was so enchanting and attractive to him that the simple sweep of her reach sent an arrow through his heart.

The quality of our energy is determined by how present we are in each moment. What makes people charismatic and attractive is their aliveness—how "awake" they are. Our "efficiency" culture emphasizes the value of results, bottom lines, and end goals, but if we are always focused on the future rather than the now, the energy in whatever we are creating will be lifeless. When we are engaged with life, no matter what we're doing, we are "paid" every moment in richness and depth. If we devalue the present moment by making it solely a means to an end, the end will be tainted by our absence.

> **Trust, love, what we call sexy, who we trust in a business situation, are all based on how open we are. Openness is bodily openness, muscular relaxation, heart openness as opposed to hiding behind some emotional wall, and spiritual openness, which is actually feeling so fully into the moment that there's no separation between you and the entire moment.**
>
> **—David Deida**

Looking Ahead

Working with the Co-Creative Power of Energy in this chapter, you will learn how to lead from the passion and love in your heart, mobilize and sustain energy on demand, and be guided by your energy clues to discern what is yours to do.

By becoming more intimate with your Co-Creative Power of Energy, you will:

- Strengthen and balance your directional, dynamic energy with your softer, receptive energy
- Learn to trust and listen to your energy to guide you on your path
- Become aware of the message you send with your energy
- Find and follow what has energy in your life
- Learn ways to brighten your energy on demand (hundred-kilowatt energy!)

When we're grounded in our ego we're tapping just from our own wellspring of energy, but when we're plugged into this larger evolutionary self we actually have more drive, energy and resources available—a kind of limitless energy to do things—but it's no longer about my little agenda and my little story, its now about the great story of life unfolding, of humanity.

—Craig Hamilton

Stories

What would it be like to lead from the healthiest and strongest part of you? The essence of you that has never been hurt or wounded and is unapologetically herself? The stories that follow, my own and others, make tangible the ways in which we can lead from love—the soul's energy.

Wendy's Story: Taking the Lead

Children and animals can tell when we're sad, mad, glad, and afraid sooner than we can; they sense the energy pattern that precedes our feelings. Horses are especially tuned in. When I was ten years old I was given the choice to join Girl Scouts or take horseback riding lessons. Easy choice! My first lesson went really well. I sat proudly atop Black Beauty, feeling a special kinship and "rightness" in being partnered with this sleek, regal horse. The following week it was Janet's turn to ride Beauty, so I grudgingly climbed atop Stormy, a smaller, scruffy horse with an obvious attitude problem. As we followed the other horses circling the ring, I seethed to myself, "How come I have to have this horse?"

Suddenly a pack of dogs came out of the nearby woods and skirted the corral. Stormy lowered his head and jerked his hind-quarters up in one swift movement. I flew through the air and landed on my butt, the wind knocked out of me. From then on, whenever I was around horses I would try to cover up my fear so they wouldn't know. But they saw through me.

Ten years after the bucking incident, a friend took me to a stable to go trail riding. Fifteen minutes out, my horse decided to lie down and rub his back on the ground (with me still in the saddle). The next time (years later) I reluctantly mounted a horse, it wouldn't move at all.

Two decades later when I had the opportunity to attend an "Equine Leadership" course presented by Ariana Strozzi of Sky-horse Ranch, I hesitated. But my curiosity won me over.

Ariana took our group of twenty women outside to the fenced-in arena and discussed how the principles of horseman-ship parallel the principles of leadership. She introduced us to her beautiful mare, Catalyst, and explained that humans didn't invent leadership—the animal kingdom arrived at it long ago as a way social animals self-organize. Unlike typical human leadership mod-els, however, horses don't create a dominant-subordinate rela-tionship (boss-to-direct-report); they know that every member has a role. The lead mare's role is simply to set direction. She earns that authority by being very sure of herself. She doesn't wonder, "Should we go this way or that?" "Should we run?" She acts decisively and the herd follows instinctively. The male lead's role is to pull the pack together because stragglers become vulnerable. He basically says, "Do what she says." What a concept!

As we began our leadership exercise, Ariana directed each of us to set an intention by declaring what we wanted to bring forth into the world: write a book, start a business, create a rela-tionship, and so on. Then we took turns entering the arena, tak-ing Catalyst's "lead"—the term for a long line attached to her halter—and asking her to first walk, then trot, then canter in a circle around us. Because horses make decisions based on what they energetically sense, not what they think, the horse's behavior served as a metaphor (and an uncanny feedback device) reflecting how committed each of us was to our stated intention.

Ariana told us that as you walk up to horses, they are assessing: "Are you gonna lead me or am I gonna lead you?" They want to know, "What do you care about?" and "Are you committed to it?" She coached us to connect with and lead Catalyst from our "hara," or belly, the seat of our spiritual energy—where our authentic power resides. The horse would read our energy, emotions, and body language and respond to how firmly rooted we were in our own inner authority.

For many of us, it was one of the most powerful and unforgettable leadership experiences ever. The horse offered instant and personal feedback to each of us; every single woman had different results. Kathy tried to sweet-talk the horse, making little clicking sounds and baby talking: "C'mon, sweetie, you can do it." Nicole barked orders and stomped her feet, which elicited a "so what?" glance from the horse. If we were uncertain or inauthentic, Catalyst seemed to say, "I'm not interested in you," or "No way, to go with you would be unsafe." Barbara couldn't get the horse to move an inch, so she started pulling and trying to drag her forward. Without realizing it, we were each revealing our approach to life.

Then it was my turn. I wasn't sure what to expect. I dug down to the energy in my belly and sent a message to the heart of this magnificent horse: Let's do this! To my astonishment, Catalyst followed my lead and walked around me, then trotted, then cantered. I could feel in my body what it was to really lead. I was firm but also relational. Instead of "me" and "you," I thought "we." Instead of dominating, I was committed—both to relationship and to action. I finally learned what it felt like to take the lead, not conceptually, but from my core.

You are destined for greatness that begins with your believing in your own destiny.

—Mary Morrissey

Tyra's Story: Popping the Cork

Tyra's nomination to president of the board of a prestigious national organization brought up mixed feelings. She had a strong track record of producing results and was thrilled about the recognition and the opportunity to play at a new level. She just wasn't sure she could lead this executive team to where they needed to go next.

Tyra had always relied on her masculine strengths—her drive and skills—for success. She was the first person in seven years to put her organization's strategic plan in place. She knew how to streamline systems, interpret financials, and get things done. But her energy was sometimes stilted and staccato—as if held captive by an inner restraint.

Early in our coaching, Tyra told me that as a young girl she had failed to make the cheerleading squad. This early rejection branded the belief in her that she would "never have the right clothes, the right friends, or the right stuff." This defining mindset spurred Tyra to try harder to compensate for her perceived lack. She had chipped away at this fear-based identity as she rose to leadership in every job she held. But even with all that she had accomplished, she often felt something working against her. Even the simple request to her boss for an increase in her department's budget brought up thoughts like "I'm not a success" or "I'm not a good manager." These limiting beliefs restrained Tyra's energy. The board needed cohesion and inspiration; they needed to be galvanized behind a compelling vision. To get real buy-in from her constituents, Tyra would need to convey the energy of certainty, passion, and unbridled enthusiasm.

Fortunately, Tyra's desire to make a difference was bigger than her story, bigger than her past, bigger than her fears. Calling in an opportunity that was worthy of her potential demanded that her energy rise to fill it. The nomination to president of the board was Tyra's moment to embody her power and natural strength as a leader.

She realized how long she had tamped down and suppressed that bountiful, overflowing, uninhibited energy that we are before we start colluding with the idea that we're not good enough. We all seek wholeness. Tyra's authentic self longed to blow the lid off of her structured style and express her boldness, spontaneity, and joy.

I had Tyra take out the Inner Vow she had created in the Spiral Up! course. As she read it aloud, the words that most reverberated were: "I am a cheerleader for women and myself." Her widened eyes met mine as she realized the thread of her life purpose. From this new vantage point, we took stock of all the ways Tyra had already proven her success, including heading up the women's organization within her corporation and supporting and championing hundreds of women in their careers and lives. Beyond bolstering her self-esteem, taking stock put Tyra in touch with the love she had for bringing out the best in others.

By acknowledging and owning her accomplishments and standing in her passion for empowering others, Tyra transformed her hesitancy into an effervescent energy. The cork finally popped, and the real Tyra was flowing free.

At the next board meeting, Tyra arrived early and decorated the room with streamers. She placed vases of beautiful flowers and bowls of fresh fruit on the table. Her opening remarks were filled with gratitude for the opportunity to serve and an appreciation for the group. She asked all members to show up at a new level, in service of the audacious vision they held for the company. Tyra had found her way into true leadership not through control but by leading people to the place in themselves where they experienced their own power and brilliance. Best of all, she realized that she didn't need to do this alone. She was part of a wonderful community with a shared vision.

When we cultivate a relationship with what we love—whether it's our family, our pet, our customers, or life itself—we eradicate fear and feelings of insignificance. As Tyra told me, "When I think about my bigger calling, all pettiness and fear fade away and I know I am unstoppable. I am empowered! And I know I'm not alone."

Your task is not to seek for love, but merely to seek and find all the barriers within yourself that you have built against it.

—Attributed to Rumi

Exercises

Use the exercises here to track the flow of energy through your life, listen compassionately to the parts of you that are resistant or fearful, and heed the call to do what has energy for you.

What Makes Your River Flow?

As we find and follow what has energy, as we support ourselves in transforming again and again, we become energized and enlivened. We open like a riverbed for more of our gifts and beauty to flow through. But how do you align with the call of the universe? How do you discover what the universe wants for you? By noticing what you feel called to do. The best example of this is a peak experience: a time when your energy flows with passion, focus, and vibrancy—when you literally feel on top of the world.

1. **Think of a "peak" work experience.** Examples: successfully pulled off a challenging project, built a great team, was recognized for my contribution.

2. **In the selected "peak" experience, what function did you serve?** Examples: coordinated an initiative, checked facts or figures, mentored others.

3. **What specifically did you contribute or accomplish to make it a peak experience?**
Examples: collaboration, a great idea, a product or service.

4. **What in you allowed for that—what skills, abilities, passions, gifts?** Examples: my passion for the people or project, influencing skills, problem solving.

5. Recall and write about three different peak experiences. What or who was present? What were you doing? What attracted you to the opportunity? Is there a theme that connects them? What does this tell you about your soul's true purpose?

When you do things from your soul, you feel a river moving in you, a joy.

—Rumi

Divine Discernment

When you're endeavoring to take on something new, it's common to meet inner resistance. If you find yourself in that inner "no," or struggling with procrastination, worry, negativity, or doubt, remember this: the ego's job is to try to talk us out of anything that might shake up the status quo or threaten our self-image. In fact, expect it! The closer your ambitions are to your soul's evolution, the more powerful the level of resistance we encounter. When (not if) you meet resistance, please don't succumb to its downward pull. Remember, resistance is not personal. There are times, however, where there is wisdom in your "inner no" and a good reason not to act. In the Third Turning, you are becoming skillful at distinguishing whether your resistance is your energy's wise guidance or the ego's lament.

The next time you have contradictory feelings about an opportunity, try to drop below your thinking self to your body's energy wisdom.

Journal the answers to these questions:

Is my resistance a form of fear?
What is my energy trying to tell me?
Is there something else I need to know to go forward?
What do I need to know to feel an inner "yes"?

Establishing Your Leadership Presence

Try this energy experiment: allow your body to slump over and try to exclaim, "I am a leader!" It's almost impossible when your posture is sending out such a contradictory energy message.

The way we hold our bodies shapes our energy and predisposes us to certain thoughts. When we shift our energy, it changes the way our mind perceives. Aikido master and Conscious Embodiment teacher Wendy Palmer says that when we slouch or slump, we cue our "personality" self, which is prone to irritations and feels an ongoing low-grade threat. This constricted posture triggers thoughts of comparing, judging, and fixing.

On the other hand, when we sit tall, lengthening our core, and take slow, deep breaths, we call on our connection to heaven and earth. We see the "big picture" and access the truth that we are all in this together.

Catching our tendency to droop and constrict gets at a more fundamental level of change than any amount of thinking can. When we notice and attend to our body's posture, our energy changes and we transform.

Highlights

- To lead more powerfully, call upon confident, dynamic energy together with the energy of love and connection.
- No matter what we're doing, if we are fully engaged with life, it stokes our energy.
- The energy of an inner "no" can transform into a resounding "yes!" if we meet it with compassion and curiosity.
- Our energy lifts simply when we think about an idea or direction that is right for us.
- Consciously attending to our breath and posture develops leadership presence.

CHAPTER 14

Let Your Divine Mind Inspire
You to Greatness

The Co-Creative Power of Mind

**Most of us think of the mind as a mirror more or less
accurately reflecting what is outside of us and not realizing that the mind itself is the principle element of
creation.**

—Rabindranath Tagore

"The future belongs to a very different kind of person with a very different
kind of mind," writes workplace expert Dan Pink in *A Whole New Mind*. "The
era of 'left brain' dominance, and the Information Age that it engendered,
are giving way to a new world in which 'right brain' qualities—inventiveness,
empathy, meaning—predominate."

In other words, if we're going to change the world, we're going to have to
change the way we think. To evolve from our small self to our greater inspired
self depends in large part on how skillful we become at using our Co-Creative
Power of Mind to balance the two different sides of our brain. It's easy to frit-
ter our days away in our transactional, left-brain "ticktock" reality. This is
the reality we spend most of our time in. In this chapter, however, you'll discover what's possible when we allow our "right mind" to inform our actions,
and you'll also be inspired by stories of extraordinary women whose lives and
courage epitomize that thrilling shift.

And as you go through the remaining chapters in this final Turning of the Spiral, you'll experience how all your Co-Creative Powers synergize to help you get in your "right mind."

The Divine Mind Within

Dr. Jill Bolte Taylor, a stroke survivor and brain researcher who lost and then recovered the function of her left brain, tells us that our ultimate goal is to have a balanced brain and to call on the skills of each side equally. Our left hemisphere gives us the capacity for language, along with our ability to think sequentially, methodically, and linearly and communicate with the external world. Our right hemisphere is our big-picture capacity, our context for everything. It affords us more nuanced kinds of understanding. Dr. Taylor explains that the right brain is our "intuition, it's our witness or our observer, it's our ability to experience deep inner peace."

Our Western society favors the left brain. Our dominant left-brain orientation is what ancient philosophers called "dualism" because from this perspective we perceive reality as the coexistence of opposites: black/white, us/them, right/wrong, life/death, good/bad, and so on. Dualistic thinking helps us make crucial distinctions, yet it limits us by dismissing anything that doesn't fit into what we currently believe or understand—anything that is new, mysterious, or threatening.

According to Dr. Taylor, it is the left brain that is most often in charge. "Your thoughts are created by a tiny, tiny little group of cells about the size of a peanut sitting in your left hemisphere. Many of us let that little peanut rule our lives." This part of our brain helps us make sense out of experiences by labeling, comparing, classifying, and categorizing—we need our ego's left-brained thinking to get from point A to point B and out the door in the morning—but often these left-brain thoughts narrowly and detrimentally define us. If we're not careful, they can create rigid walls for a boxed-in life: *I'm shy. I'm a good girl. I'm responsible.* Often, compounding these beliefs is an underlying soundtrack: That's the best I can do. I'm a loser. I'll never change. I can't do it. These assumptions and beliefs compose our life's blueprint and, if left unquestioned, dictate who we become.

Our right brain, on the other hand, gives us access to what philosophers of Eastern cosmologies call non-duality, a state of being in which there is no sense of separation between the observer and what is being observed. This might be hard to grasp intellectually, but we've all experienced it briefly, in nature, making love, or meditating, or even over a meal with good friends. This right-brain consciousness awakens us to the profound truth of our connection and interdependence with everything. Only in this softer space of "non-dual thinking" do we experience open-heartedness and inner peace and connect with the biggest picture of all, universal consciousness and the divine mind within. It is here that we are present to the "vertical realm," where dreams, insight, and divine direction bubble up from our wisest self.

All great religions seek to give us methods for detaching from obsessive-compulsive thought so that we may realize our vastness. But in its effort to keep us living horizontally, the left brain cancels out some of what the right brain offers.

Don't Believe Everything You Think

We allow good to come to us in direct proportion to our sense of self-worth. In fact, we never take an action inconsistent with who we think ourselves to be. And yet our self-image and self-esteem are often derived from misinformation. Our left brain, or dualistic mind, sorts, selects, and interprets information based on how it affects our ego's cares and concerns, not our soul's. These fixed ideas and stories live invisible to us as our reality.

Take Meg, who lived with the story that professional achievement and material success would make her happy. Zealously following the traditional "success" trajectory, she reached a level of financial and professional accomplishment that would make a CEO swoon. But when her considerable achievements left her with a hollow feeling, it spurred a painful wake-up call. Fortunately, it was what she needed for her "right mind" to be heard.

Upsetting experiences can serve us by destabilizing our egos long enough to allow something new in. Meg's "right mind" afforded her a glimpse of truth from what I call her "penthouse consciousness"—the higher view. She realized, "It's really who I am and what I stand for that's important to me. I have gifts and a desire to share those. I want to be present. I want to be conscious."

When we're in our "right mind," we don't need an explanation for everything. Meg simply knew she needed to pursue a more meaningful path. But her left brain wasn't about to give up so easily. In fact, whenever we make a choice to follow our soul's calling, our ego will challenge and test us. On one day in particular, Meg's thoughts tormented her. She compared herself unfavorably to a very successful younger woman, a mover and shaker who was more driven, more accomplished, and on a fast track to more financial and professional rewards.

Meg felt the familiar pang of her self-accusatory thoughts: "You're not keeping up!" Yet, because of her right brain's elevated awareness, she was able to question her left brain's harsh judgment. She asked herself, "Do I really want what Sarah has?" In a flash, Meg heard her truth: "I've seen her life up close. I'm not interested in it." Instead, Meg was committed to using her appreciable skills and creative talents to start her own company that contributed to transformational, large-scale change. Now, fully on her own side, Meg could enlist her left brain's practical and logistical know-how to support her inspired vision.

When we reach outside our patterns and fixed ways of thinking and have faith in what we can't yet see, we evolve. To align with our soul's vision, we don't use our left-brain "figuring out" skills as much as our feminine gift of receiving and sensing. Our right brain is the gateway that connects us with our true "I" through our imagination, intuition, and ideas. The word *idea* comes from the Greek *idein*, meaning "to see." It's our contemplative "right mind" that gives us a transcendent view, letting us see the subtle vision of our dreams before they have fully taken shape in our lives.

> **Everything is practice when you're in your right mind.**
> **—Joan Halifax**

Looking Ahead

Working with the Co-Creative Power of Mind in this chapter, you will put into practice the core principles for seeing, knowing, and manifesting what you really want.

As you practice living from your "right mind," you will:

- Attune to your intuition's subtle guiding messages
- Interrupt and uplift negative thoughts more quickly
- Become more conscious and intentional as you go through your day
- Be inspired to conceive of and believe in your limitless potential
- Allow the boundlessness of your Divine Mind to inspire you to greatness

Stories

Let the stories that follow speak to you of the force of dreams, the vital connection between the mind and the heart, and the power of deep conviction to bring a new future within reach.

Lisa's Story: Clarity of Heart

Lisa's warmth reached me even before we shook hands. Her smiling, inquisitive eyes were even more striking than her six-foot frame clad in a beautiful bespoke jacket. George, from the outsourcing company that had referred her to me, had written that Lisa was a forty-something superstar at a large media firm in the New York area. Her position had been eliminated in a recent reorganization. Since she was an accomplished executive with a twenty-year tenure in a highly competitive industry, I was immediately impressed by how she had managed to stay so humble and good-humored.

Lisa told me she was from the Midwest, a possible factor contributing to her gracious spirit. Her roots also lent a hint as to why, without so much as a month off, she accepted a job with another firm; she herself attributed it to those heartland "buck up, work hard" values. But I sensed there were other, less visible dynamics that played into her hasty decision.

Lisa liked the novelty of being a big fish in a little pond, which her new job with a start-up gave her. But she hadn't anticipated such a chaotic and disorganized culture. Four months into the assignment she wanted to leave. "It lacks the right kind of challenge," Lisa told me. She was already considering two markedly different opportunities.

The first thing I wondered aloud was, "What's the rush?" Her first company had provided her with a generous severance package that included six months' salary. With the addition of her new job, she was bringing in the pay of two people. Lisa agreed that it was time to slow down and examine what she really wanted.

It's better to be pulled toward a future because we want it rather than to be pushed into it out of fear of what will happen if we say no. I asked Lisa what motivated her decision to take the job with the start-up. She admitted that her loudest thoughts at the time were, "I'm the sole breadwinner for my family. Maybe I won't get a better offer. I don't want to become irrelevant." Although it lurked beneath the surface, fear had also played a part in the fact that she had rarely taken a vacation in her twenty-year-plus career.

As we explored multiple opportunities, Lisa told me that she was considering a job in executive recruitment. Lisa was comfortable with senior executives, as well as the limousines and expense accounts that often came with that line of work. Despite her seeming enthusiasm, I invited her to examine her true priorities.

From a deck of cards representing different values, Lisa selected the ones that mattered most in her life: "staying healthy," "inner peace," "work/life balance," and "making a difference." As she absorbed her choices, Lisa's eyes widened. She knew immediately that the competitive and frantic-paced headhunter business would not be a fit and that the other choice would.

Not everyone arrives at a revelation that course-corrects life so swiftly, but clarity can happen in a heartbeat when we "feel into" a situation rather than just thinking about it. Instead of going for the fast-paced, buttoned-down, glam world of big business she had grown up in, Lisa accepted the opportunity to run a division of a socially responsible firm, just a bicycle ride from home. She could apply her breadth of experience to support this fledgling company and be at her nine-year-old son's soccer matches!

It is easy to be swayed by the relentless messages of fear, cynicism, and mistrust that pervade our airwaves. But if you're a loyal listener to the "fear station," you'll stay frozen in place. To flourish we must attune to what inspires us and to the deeper truth and wisdom of our hearts. In many Asian languages, the words for *mind* and *heart* are the same. When we connect head with heart our lives unfold from the inside out.

Fear is just a negative thought.

—Byron Katie

Lynne's Story: The Power of Dreams

I had tea recently with a very special woman I've known and deeply admired for three decades—Lynne Twist, a global activist and author of *The Soul of Money*. She shared a story with me about a group of Senegalese women who dreamed a very power-ful dream—one that would eventually lead to healing for a small region of West Africa.

In 1980, in her capacity as founder of the Hunger Project, Lynne took a group of donors to Senegal, Africa. Their destina-tion was Thies, the last city of any size before reaching the Sahel Desert. The Sahel, expanding as a result of drought, harbored a growing number of distressed people who had no water. Lynne's group was going in search of them.

"Soon the road disappeared beneath the sand," Lynne told me. "We were in a dust bowl, everybody covered in a film of fine orange dust. In the absence of a road, the driver of the lead Land Rover turned the jeeps toward the sound of drums beating in the distance. Soon black specks appeared on the horizon. As they got closer and the specks got bigger, we realized they were children—about a hundred running towards our vehicles."

The children jumped on the running boards and on top of the jeeps and guided the group to a place where a large baobab tree stood, under which two hundred people sat. They were from a string of seventeen villages that were in desperate straits. Lack of water was taking the lives of as many as five people a day, mostly little children. They brought Lynne's group to the nearest village, where they met with the village chief and the mullahs of the Muslim villages. The men sat in a circle, and since Lynne was the leader of the delegation, even though she was a woman, they allowed her into the circle along with her translator. The men told Lynne of their desperate circumstances, the direness of their situa-tion overwhelming. The next day another circle formed to discuss what might be done. This time, however, a group of women from the villages sat right behind Lynne, in what she told me felt like "a clump of feminine power."

Lynne described the women as beautiful, dressed in bright fabrics and veils. As Lynne listened intently to the tribesmen's con-cerns, one woman began to inch forward toward the circle. "She scooted up behind me and I could feel her. I turned around and looked at her and then moved over just a little bit. She moved closer and I shifted to make a very small space between the next man and me. Suddenly she was sitting in the circle. I could feel the power shift. I could feel the truth of what I later found out: that no woman (aside from me—a white foreigner) had ever been included in that circle."

After the meeting, Lynne asked permission of the chief and the mullahs to meet with the women, accompanied by her translator. The women squealed with excitement when they heard that they would be talking with Lynne. Slowly, more and more women joined the circle, and then they shared with Lynne what their divine wisdom told them: beneath the village there was an underground lake so large it possibly extended to two or three other villages. The women told Lynne they knew the lake existed beyond a doubt because they could feel it in their hearts and because more and more of them dreamed of it each night.

The men thought it was folly, and the women weren't allowed to dig for water without permission. Even so, they wouldn't give up. The lake existed—their dreams and hearts told them so.

This, then, was the Hunger Project's task: to get the agreement of the chiefs and mullahs for the women to dig for water. That accomplished, the women began to dig. They began with their hands and the rudimentary tools they had; later, they used tools the Hunger Project provided: shovels, buckets, ropes, ladders. They did this for more than a year, even as they fed their families and worked their farms, sustained by only tiny amounts of emergency water that the government provided, and that only at the insistence of the Hunger Project.

Because the women believed so strongly in their dreams, their conviction and courage were unrelenting. After months of hard labor, they hit water—a deep and vast underground lake that stretched for miles.

When Lynne returned to the village years later, she found it transformed. Storage towers bulged with food, and women were taking out small loans and selling surplus goods at the local market. The children were no longer hungry, thirsty, or dying. More than seventy-five thousand people were living a decent life. Because they believed in their dreams, the women had brought healing not just to their village, but to the whole region.

As I listened to Lynne tell me her extraordinary story, I was reminded once again how essential it is to listen to our divine wisdom—however it comes to us. For the women of the Sahel, heeding their dreams was a matter of life and death. For us as well, at least on a spiritual or psychological level, tuning in to our inner knowing through our dreams, our hopes, and our intuition can be the wellspring for a rich and meaningful life.

Exercises

Use the exercises here to try on a new mind-set, break out of the "boxes" that confine you, interrupt the thoughts that cause a downward spiral, and call on the wisdom of your inner knowing to answer your deepest questions.

Walls into Bridges!

I think God has a sense of humor. For years I searched for my life's purpose and then one day realized it had always been right in front of me: Wallbridge. My name embodied my passion for transformation—turning walls into bridges—so that people move past obstacles, change their destiny, and live from their authentic calling. One way that we wall ourselves in is by giving ourselves labels: "senior manager," "starving artist," "breadwinner." These labels contain and limit us, creating neat and tidy definitions that separate us from the magnificent and unlimited ocean of potentiality that is our true nature. Who you desire to be is outside your current identity.

Take, for example, this story of Edward Adamson, an English art therapist. He asked a group of young people to look at a brick and write down as many ideas as they could think of for how to use it. Some of the children had hundreds of ideas, but many of them struggled to think of more than a few. Adamson asked those children to close their eyes and imagine that they were great artists known for their creative bravery and talent. With this new perspective, as clever, imaginative, creative geniuses, the children came up with an abundance of ideas for the brick's use. All because of the way they saw themselves—as "artists."

So imagine how you might describe yourself if you couldn't use those familiar and limiting labels. Imagine if you actually had to think of yourself as something bigger, grander, more unlimited. Examples: I am a beacon of inspiration for women to rise, I am a lover of creativity who lives to make beauty, I am the one who brings joy and ease to every situation.

What word or phrase could you use to define yourself that would free you to live the grandest possible version of yourself?

Once you have your phrase, write it down and place it somewhere you can read it every day.

> I am larger, better than I thought,
> I did not know I held so much goodness.
>
> —Walt Whitman

Trust Your Intuition

In a rapidly changing environment women's intuitive strengths, like our ability to read the tea leaves, peer around corners, and be predictive, are highly valued competencies for innovative companies. These feminine strengths don't belong to one gender, but are a new form of competitive advantage for today's world. As Lynne's story illustrates, the feminine strength of receptivity enables women to tap into a wealth of information not always available to our more rational and analytic selves. Once dismissed as pure fancy, this ability to act on our gut feelings is increasingly being seen as a critical asset. So how can you begin to trust and honor your deeper knowing?

1. Keep an intuition journal. Track your "gut feelings" over time and notice how often your intuitive self is "right on."
2. Create a dream circle. Invite a group of women to come together on a regular basis to share your dreams with each other.
3. Make a commitment to take action on at least one of your intuitive insights.

Treat as existent already that which you yearn for, that which you long for, that which you would most want to bring into the world to experience and express. It is existent in the first realm of cause, which is the creative chamber of your own thinking.

—Mary Morrissey

Stand in the Regard Others Have for You

In Mary Morrisey's book, *Building Your Field of Dreams*, she writes, "Many years ago, my mentor asked if I thought it possible that the ten-year plan we'd devised to establish a church home could be manifested in a single year. I told him no. So he asked if I could believe that he believed it possible. To this question, I answered yes. What he told me next was: 'Then believe in my belief.' These words opened the door to a miracle, and indeed, our church home was established not ten years, but ten months later."

We all need a trusted friend or advisor to believe for us when we cannot do it on our own. Who might that person be for you? Think of three people who hold you in high regard. What would be possible if you gave credence to the virtues and strengths that they see in you?

Just take responsibility for the thoughts you're thinking and move yourself into the circuitry that brings you peace. You have to teach yourself when you're there so that you can identify what it feels like inside your body so you can call upon it at any time.

—Dr. Jill Bolte Taylor

Highlights

- You don't have to believe your thoughts.
- Our "thinking mind" isn't who we are.
- What we "think" we want isn't always what we really want.
- To transform we must break out of our often invisible, self-imposed boxes.
- When we expand who we think we are, miracles become possible.
- We bring our dreams to life by believing in their possibility.

CHAPTER 15

The Radical Riches of Relatedness

The Co-Creative Power of Feelings

Love is the ultimate truth at the heart of creation. It is not a sentiment or an emotion—it's the fact that we're all the same being in different disguises.
—Deepak Chopra

I recommend a daily dose of Ellen DeGeneres. She keeps us in stitches, in a sweet and heartfelt way. Deepak Chopra was once a guest on her show. Noting all the fun Ellen was instigating, Deepak said, "If we looked at the people in your audience right now, at their neurotransmitters, they would have high levels of opiates: oxytocin—the 'bonding' hormone—and all kinds of chemicals that actually fine-tune their immune system. Just the fact that they are experiencing this energy, joy, and laughter is causing their chemistry to totally change. You're actually reversing their aging!" Ellen looked at her audience and deadpanned, "You're welcome."

Spiraling up into the third level of the Co-Creative Power of Feelings has everything to do with living from our hearts, opening to let life touch us, and fully showing up to give and receive love and joy. These are the radical riches of relatedness.

I discovered this again for myself just recently. At the close of every year, I do a "completion review" to make space for the brand-new year to be born. This year, what stood out for me was that my most pleasurable, rewarding experiences—my high points—had to do with connection: connection with spirit, connection with friends and loved ones, connection with clients, and connection with nature.

If you recall the last time your heart was touched, moved, or inspired, it's likely that it too was triggered by your connection with others: perhaps a tender moment with a loved one; the plight of natural disaster victims or the tireless workers coming to their aid; or something as innocent as a YouTube link to an astonishing heavenly voice unleashed upon a skeptical audience. These "mind-blowing" moments drop us into our hearts.

Only connect.

—**E. M Forster**

The "In Between"

According to Jonathan Haidt, PhD, associate professor in social psychology at the University of Virginia, "Human happiness derives neither from external validation nor solely from within, but from 'between.'" In other words, it's engagement that creates our sense of happiness.

Can you recall a moment when a toddler reached up to you with a wide-open smile? Or a flirtatious kitten rolled on her back to invite a belly rub? When we drop into our hearts in moments such as these, it's as if a current runs between us and the other being, pulling us toward each other. This is the current of love; we are joined by the deeper truth of our hearts.

These moments of intimacy can happen daily—with our spouses, partners, or pets. If we're lucky, we may also feel this deep sense of communion with a special piece of land, beloved tree, or ancient rock. Joy, compassion, and gratitude are all emotions that are born of love. And loving isn't something we do in isolation. We embody love—we are love—when we open our hearts for others to enter.

Classical societies had a special term for it: *aesthesis*, which means "to breathe in." Author Stephen Buhner writes, "They [the Greeks] recognized that the moment of touch was accompanied by a gasp, a particular kind of inspiration. They considered it the moment when the soul essence inside us, and the soul essence from something outside us, met and mingled." This mingling of our soul essences is supported through science. Brain-imaging research shows that when we observe someone drinking a glass of water, the same neurons light up in our brain as if we were the ones drinking. When we see somebody in pain, we feel as if we are in pain. Because our nervous system mimics what we observe, this gives us more compassion and understanding for others' actions and motivations. Our neurocircuitry is interwoven with others. We are inextricably linked.

There is no time not to love.

—**Deena Metzger**

To Be Happy, Know Yourself

In order to access the joy that's available to us in the "in between," we have to make another essential connection—within ourselves, with our own hearts. Dr. Robert Holden, the author of *Happiness Now! Timeless Wisdom for Feeling Good Fast* and director of the Happiness Project, says, "The reason why we're so interested in happiness is because we want to have an experience of our true self. You feel happiest when you begin to get to know who you truly are." Real happiness is your original nature, always available to you, and, as Holden says, "the more true you are to yourself, the happier you'll be."

Meditation is a primary way to access happiness simply because it invites the most important of all connections—to our original nature, our inner selves. Richie Davidson, PhD, of "Science of Happiness" fame, performed a study with Buddhist monks, "the Olympic athletes of meditation," as he calls them. Davidson conducted MRI brain scans on monks as they meditated on what Buddhists call the Four Divine Attitudes: loving kindness, compassion, empathetic joy, and peace or equanimity. As the monks held these ideas in deep contemplation, brain imaging showed dramatic changes in their decision-making and social "control" center, the prefrontal cortex, which flooded with healthy "well-being" chemicals. Surprisingly, the areas involving motor planning were also affected. The monks didn't just feel better; their brains were preparing their bodies to jump into action in service of others.

Davidson's studies confirm the brain's plasticity, showing that with a little training, even if we have a predisposition to anxiety or depression, it's possible to change our "emotional set point" and increase our capacity to experience more happiness. What that means is that happiness is generative. The more we feel it, the more our brains are inclined to invite us to feel it again.

Spiraling Up Our Feelings

Underneath our civilized personas lurks a wide variety of feelings, both dark and light. Our darker feelings, such as anger, disdain, jealousy, disgust, resentment, or intolerance, may rarely see the light of day because they seem less acceptable. Yet if we suppress negative feelings, we will unconsciously project them outward, causing suffering. When we can fully receive and work with feelings as they arise—as we practiced in the Second Turning in the Co-Creative Power of Feelings—we learn to integrate difficult emotions and return more rapidly to our natural state of peace and contentment.

It's impossible to overstate the importance of this: there is well-established research on the debilitating effects of negativity and stress, and more recently, compelling evidence has begun to illuminate the bounty of benefits available from feeling good. I've read extensively in this new area of research, and in the process I've developed a list of key points. Take a look at what I call the "Six Miraculous Merits" of joy, happiness, and love:

1. Our brain chemistry changes for the better, much as Richie Davidson discovered. Deepak Chopra's book *Reinventing the Body, Resurrecting the Soul: How to Create a New You* cites breakthrough discoveries, such as how happiness increases production of neurotransmitters—chemicals that serve as antidepressants, enhance self-esteem, and fine-tune the activity of the immune system, which protects us from infections and illnesses like cancer.

2. Our genes get healthier. There are five hundred genes that influence things like heart disease, inflammation, obesity, and some types of cancer. These genes are pliant. Chopra says that we can turn the good genes on and the bad genes off in just three months with adjustments to diet and attitude— in particular, by experiencing the "intoxication of love."

3. Our sense of trust and social well-being increases. In *Born to Be Good: The Science of a Meaningful Life*, Dacher Keltner, professor of psychology at UC Berkeley, shares that when someone smiles at us, our heart rate and blood pressure go down. And because we usually smile back, we benefit from the release of dopamine, the pleasure-producing chemical in the brain, which in turn invites connection, warmth, a sense of calm, and intimacy.

4. We act altruistically. Good feelings increase our capacity to feel and do good. Researchers at the University of Wisconsin found that after just six weeks of meditating on loving kindness, software engineers showed increased immune function and significant activation in the left frontal lobes of their brains, the region that supports compassionate action.

5. We tap into creativity. Positive feelings broaden the range of our thinking and actions. We see and think of more options to solve whatever problem we face. According to the *Journal of Neuroscience*, when we're in a good mood, our visual cortex becomes more peripheral; we take in more information, and possibilities abound. Bad moods, on the other hand, result in tunnel vision.

6. We create an upward spiral. Psychologists say that positive emotions help us to see favorable meaning in all events and circumstances. When we feel that everything happens to us for a good reason, our feelings uplift, creating a self-reinforcing cycle. Fueled by gratitude, love, appreciation, or compassion, we look for the opportunity behind every challenge—and Spiral Up!

The Moon in Our Eyes

At one of our "Sweat Your Prayers" movement classes, our teacher Lori took a minute to honor one of our dancemates who had unexpectedly passed. She held up his photograph, saying, "Whenever Eric greeted me, he always made me feel like I was his special teacher. When I told this to Kathy [her co-teacher], Kathy said, 'That's funny. I always felt special when Eric and I connected as well.'"

Smiling at us, Lori said, "What a wonderful thing to be able to say about someone, that whenever he greeted you, he made you feel like you were a long-lost friend. That is the essence of love."

Lori then read us this poem by the fourteenth-century Persian poet Hafiz:

Admit something:
Everyone you
see, you say to them, "Love me."
Of course you do not do this out loud,
otherwise someone would call the cops.
Still, though, think about this, this great pull in us to connect.
Why not become the one who lives with a full moon in each eye
that is always saying,
with that sweet moon language,
what every other eye in this world
is dying
to hear?

Lori concluded, "When I die I want to be fully engaged, riveted, living and dancing with full-heartedness." She instructed us to "live and dance with full hearts; dance with the moon in your eyes!"

The highest level of the Co-Creative Power of Feelings supports us in living full out, undefended, all in, giving and receiving love. Being happy is a choice we make day to day, hour to hour, and moment to moment. When we become disciples of "feeling good," we manage our thoughts, feelings, words, and actions so that they uplift and give birth to a positive future. We learn to dance with the moon in our eyes.

Looking Ahead

As you work with the Co-Creative Power of Feelings in this chapter, you will be inspired to live from your heart, open to let life touch you, and fully show up to give and receive love.

As you practice the radical riches of relatedness, you will:

- Feel joy, compassion, forgiveness, and connection more frequently
- Learn to use your thoughts to bring your emotions into balance
- Get skillful at turning around downward spirals
- Become attractive to what you want and more accessible to others

> **Can you tolerate happiness? If we don't believe ourselves worthy of happiness, we won't allow love to take root in our lives. It's outside of our beliefs about our lives and we'll sabotage love.**
>
> **—Nathaniel Branden**

Stories

As you explore the Co-Creative Power of Feelings to its fullest, let yourself be inspired by these stories of giving and forgiving, cultivating connection and compassion, and opening the heart in sometimes surprising ways.

Susan's Story: Open Your Heart and Live

When we last saw Susan, she had just returned from a Zen retreat where she had healed the grief of her sister's death. This transformative experience had awakened a deep calling in her to serve others.

Though still unclear on how to answer the call, Susan felt pressure to get a job. She reworked her résumé, networked, and went on job interviews. After two months, Susan accepted a position with a bank that offered the opportunity for worldwide travel, something she had always wished for. As she readied for a trip, she noticed her zafu pillow abandoned in a corner.

She hadn't meditated in over a year.

She lifted a stack of papers, and her journal from the Buddhist retreat fell to the floor. The tea-stained cover brought back conversations in the zendo's kitchen and her deep desire to help people in their living and dying. Later that week, another nudge came as she read an article about Laurie, a woman who had created Jacob's Heart, an organization for kids with cancer. She couldn't ignore the tug at her own heart. Susan thought, "I feel called to this kind of work, but let's face it, I'm avoiding it. I'm still uncomfortable being with dying people but it's time I did something. At the very least I could help raise money for these kids."

She arranged to meet Laurie for lunch. An energetic New Yorker, Laurie had enough enthusiasm for both of them. Before Susan knew it, she had agreed to help with the rounds of visits at the hospital that day. Entering the Lucile Packard Children's Hospital, Susan quaked. She diverted her eyes to the bags of small gifts she was carrying and told herself, "Just breathe."

As they entered the oncology department, Laurie walked briskly past a set of private rooms. Trailing behind, Susan noticed a small, thin girl sitting alone in her bed. Their eyes met. "Can we go in there?" Susan called to Laurie, who was halfway down the corridor.

Laurie responded, "It's better if we start in a different section." (Later, Susan realized that these rooms held terminal patients and Laurie was trying to protect her, a new volunteer, from heartbreak.) But there was that inner tug again: I can't walk past this girl. Susan stuck her head in the door and asked, "May I come in?"

Marisa Rojas was fourteen years old. She had big brown eyes, a captivating smile, beautiful bone structure, and curly brown hair, which, Susan found out later, came and went. Marisa immediately began interviewing Susan. "Do you have kids? How come you're here? Are you doing this as a volunteer? Do you have a regular job? Don't you have any children of your own?" After thirty minutes of interrogation, Marisa concluded, "Okay, every other kid on our floor has a mother. You're the best thing that's come along— so you'll have to do." The one family member to visit Marisa was her Mexican grandma, a migrant worker. She came when she could, but she lived far away. Marisa's real mom was an addict who lived on the streets.

For two years Marisa and Susan enjoyed the best parts of a mother–daughter relationship. Sitting side by side on Marisa's bed, they rarely missed *American Idol* or *Sabrina the Teenage Witch*. They played Yahtzee and Rummikub and talked late into the night. Their visits often revolved around Marisa's food requests: chili cheese fries, chocolate milkshakes, and her favorite treat, caramel popcorn. But even more, Marisa craved connection, and she found that with Susan. And spending time with Marisa, Susan felt an unsurpassed sense of fulfillment. Every time she walked into her room she was totally present and at peace, knowing that this was where she was supposed to be.

One afternoon Susan arrived and Marisa was still in bed. Susan sat on the edge of her mattress and stroked her small head and cheek, noticing the hair that came off in her hand. "What's up, Marisa? How are you doing today?" The chemo was taking a toll on Marisa's body and spirit. "I'm okay, just tired," she said. A surge of anger flared up in Susan's chest over the unfairness of life. "Whadda ya say we blow this joint?"

Although Marisa rarely complained, she had pestered Susan countless times to take her to the mall, "like other kids get to do." But it was against hospital rules for a child in her condition. Susan went out into the hallway and, with all of the resolve she could muster, convinced the RN on duty that this was a matter of life and death. She made a deal to have Marisa back in an hour.

When they arrived at the mall, it was Marisa who was out of the car first. "You can buy whatever you want," said Susan.

"Okay, I want a cap for my head, just no white-people colors. I want black."

Some say it was Susan's friendship that helped Marisa live a year and a half longer than anyone expected. She died just before her sixteenth birthday. Susan went on to seminary and got her master's in divinity. Today, she works in the prison system, counseling women inmates in creating new futures. When she's asked what led her to her new life, her eyes twinkle. "Marisa. In knowing her I was at my very best. I was the best I could be. I feel so lucky that I was awake when I met her. I listened to where my heart pulled me."

Love is not so much a feeling as a way of being present. Love is presence with unconditional Attention, Acceptance, Appreciation, Affection and Allowing others to be as they are.

—David Richo

One Chimp's Story: Agape, the Breaker of Chains

At this Third Turning of the Co-Creative Power of Feelings, we call forward the presence of *agape*, which in Greek means "unconditional love." Also known as "neighborly" love, agape is at the core of who we are. A love not exclusive to family and friends, agape is our capacity and impulse to feel affection for and extend loving kindness to all living beings on the planet.

In Fran Peavey's book *Heart Politics* she shares a story that illustrates the power of agape.

Fran was walking with a friend through the campus of Stanford University when she noticed a crowd with cameras and video equipment clustered on a hillside. Approaching, she saw they encircled a pair of chimpanzees—a male running loose and a female on a twenty-five-foot chain. The spectators, a mix of mostly male scientists and publicity people, were attempting to get the pair to mate. The male, eager, grunted and grabbed the female's chain and tugged. She whimpered and retreated. Each time he pulled her toward him, she pulled back.

Seeing the look on the female chimp's face, Fran felt a surge of sympathy and protection. To Fran's great surprise, the female chimp suddenly yanked her chain out of the male's grasp, walked through the crowd, straight over to Fran, and took her hand. The female chimp then led Fran across the circle to the only other two women in the crowd and joined hands with one of them.

Fran writes, "The three of us stood together in a circle. I remember the feeling of that rough palm against mine. The little chimp had recognized us and reached out across all the years of evolution to form her own support group."

What capacity allowed this frightened chimpanzee to recognize the love and support of the other women in the crowd, or for the human females to respond in kind?

There is a ribbon of love that threads through all living things, and it can be sensed and communicated beyond our own species. This kinship is seeded into our genes; kindness, friendship, romance, altruism break down barriers and bond us to each other, helping us to survive and thrive. When we're paying attention, opportunities for generosity and compassion are available and can powerfully impact us at any moment. They dissolve walls of separation, allowing tendrils of connection to swirl between us, bringing us close not only to those we know, but to strangers. Even to different species. Even to one frightened little chimp.

Remember, we all stumble, every one of us. That's why it's a comfort to go hand-in-hand.

—Emily Kimbrough

Exercises

We've seen how good for you feeling good can be. As you engage with the following exercises, you will activate all the physiological and psychological benefits of positivity, and you'll also work with negative feelings to keep them from spiraling you down.

Trusting in Love

We've experienced how opening our hearts to love can lift us up—and we all have a desire for uplift. By thinking and writing about who loves you and who or what you love, you will not only activate all the merits of positive feelings, but you'll discover that you can trust in love. While we may often stray from it, love is as natural to us and as much a part of us as breathing.

1.   **Bring to mind one person who loves you.** This could be someone in your life now or someone who has passed on, or even an ancestor whom you feel connected to. How does this person see you? Write about yourself through those loving eyes, starting with the words, *What I love about (your name) is* . . .

As you read what you have written, allow the words to fully register in every cell of your body. Let them fill you up, calm you down, open your heart, and replenish you. Repeat this journal technique from another loving person's perspective. Once you experience this several times, you will return to the natural knowing that you are loved.

2.   **What or who has a soft place in your heart?** Do you have a favorite cause, a beloved pet, or a lake, tree, or person you love?

For a simple example, I love my friend's puppy, Tipper. He is affectionate, innocent, playful, and soft.

Select someone or something that melts your heart. Open your journal and write a detailed description of the object of your affection and what you love about him, her, or it.

After you've written your piece, read through it and reflect on how easy it is for you to love. As you become more accustomed to this feeling state you will trust that not only are you loved, but you are *love*. Love is our natural state of being; it flows toward us and from us as naturally as we inhale and exhale. Even when we feel momentarily disconnected from love, it is always a part of us. We just need to learn to trust it.

"Strengthen the In-Between" Practice

In today's busy world we often zip through our days laser-focused in pursuit of our goals. In order to concentrate, we tune out our peripheral surroundings, often at the cost of new or serendipitous connections.

Imagine this is your last day on Earth. Will it matter to you how much you got done, or will you care more about how well you loved? You can expand your feelings of connection and love. Over the next few days, whether at the mall, walking down the street, or standing in line, practice bringing a more openhearted and accessible spirit to your interactions with people. See if you can let go of any guardedness to soften into a more welcoming way of being. Instead of judging people with your mind, see if you can sense the soulfulness and humanity of those you meet. Say hello or smile at someone you would not normally speak to, or simply connect in silence. Notice what you receive from that exchange.

Before you go to sleep, review any experiences of kinship or connection that you felt with another, no matter how small. Perhaps you shared a moment of friendly eye contact with a passerby. Or maybe you took time to chat with someone you ordinarily avoid, or expressed genuine interest in a family member when they called. Notice the abundance of riches available in the "in-between."

Affirm throughout your day: I open myself to fully give and receive love.

A strange passion is moving in my head.
My heart has become a bird
which searches in the sky.
Every part of me goes in different directions.
Is it really so
that the one I love is everywhere?

—Rumi

Savor the Good

Anytime you feel lured into the vortex of a downward spiral, simply bring to mind what you are grateful for. The following practice is especially powerful as a nightly ritual, and it's like money in the bank for the next time something triggers the blues.

Each night before you float off to sleep, review your day for "gratefuls." Amid the urgency of life, it's easy to lose sight of the daily instances of cooperation, kindness, and goodwill that bless our days with indescribable sweetness.

Acknowledge yourself for just one thing that you did or said today (or didn't do or say) on behalf of your intention to evolve. Next, open your heart to the people or circumstances that you feel thankful for. Allow the feelings of appreciation, love, compassion, or joy to wash over you. Revel in your good feelings. Allow them to soothe and strengthen you. See if you can magnify them. As you dwell in the positive feelings roused by these recollections, your brain will map your new circuitry. This creates a pathway for you to experience more love in your heart again and again.

The root of joy is gratefulness...It is not joy that makes
us grateful; it is gratitude that makes us joyful.

—David Steindl-Rast

Highlights

- Happiness is our original nature and a choice we make.
- Feelings of joy, happiness, and love create positive changes in brain chemistry, increase trust and social well-being, help us cope with adversity, and incline us to feel better more often.
- Until we allow loving kindness and joy into our hearts, no other goal is really worth achieving.
- Our most meaningful moments come from our connections—with loved ones, spirit, nature, and what matters to us.
- We don't so much choose our purpose as our purpose chooses us.

I am certain of nothing but the holiness of the heart's affections.

—John Keats

CHAPTER 16

Create New Worlds with Your Heartfelt Words

The Co-Creative Power of Speech

Y'all got something—find the message in it to help others.
—Robin Roberts

If you had one speech to give before you died, what would you say?

Randy Pausch, the late and brilliant Carnegie-Mellon professor, took part in a lecture series called "The Last Lecture," where professors were challenged with this question. Pausch didn't have to imagine the scenario, because just prior to the talk he was diagnosed with pancreatic cancer.

In his famous "Last Lecture," Pausch said, "My dad always taught me that when there is an elephant in the room, introduce him." He went on to share candidly and unsentimentally about his condition ("ten tumors in my liver and approximately three to six months left of good health"). The bulk of his unforgettable lecture held the crowd's rapt attention with personal, often amusing, anecdotes illuminating his lessons learned—mostly how he'd achieved his childhood dreams and enabled the dreams of others. In closing, Pausch admitted, "This talk's not for you, it's for my kids."

Every person in the room felt like they had been given a precious gift. Why? Not because they received heartfelt advice on how to lead life, but because of the intimacy Pausch created by being vulnerable and transparent.

It was this sense of intimacy that made *The Last Lecture* an Internet sensation and a best-selling book published in thirty-five languages.

The Co-Creative Power of Speech at this level invites us to open to a greater degree of vulnerability through personal and honest exchanges that dissolve boundaries and build ascending spirals of relatedness.

When we speak from the heart, we create a sacred container that transforms both speaker and listener. We create the conditions for new levels of understanding that surpass what either person could produce on her own. This is where innovation, creativity, forgiveness, and possibility are born. As if our heartfelt words had wings, they lift everyone up. In turn, when we speak about our hopes and dreams with the same unguarded sincerity, the veil is lifted between us and our desired future. Our words are both intuitive and prophetic. We lay claim to the future through speaking it in the here and now with wholeheartedness and ownership of what wants to be born through us.

The word *communication* comes from the Latin *communicare*, "to share; join, unite; to make common." The potential of communication is communion: profound relatedness and love. Real intimacy ("in-to-me-you-see") happens when we allow others a glimpse into who we really are. At this level of the Spiral, the Co-Creative Power of Speech supports us in birthing the next level of who we are by expressing our most authentic self.

> **The only currency in this bankrupt world is what you**
> **share with someone else when you're uncool.**
> **—Lester Bangs from *Almost Famous***

In-to-Me-You-See

"We're all a little like icebergs," my friend Ryland says. "Ten percent of us is above the water but the rest of us is submerged." Ryland, one of the owners of Café Gratitude in Los Angeles, opens his staff meetings with a communication exercise that "lowers the waterline." To create instant "relatedness," staff members take turns revealing something real about themselves. This act of vulnerability creates an immediate sense of connection and authenticity resulting in an energized environment and an extraordinary customer experience.

I experienced the "Iceberg Exercise" in a teleclass on authenticity with Mike Robbins, author of the book *Be Yourself, Everyone Else Is Already Taken*. Mike demonstrated the transparency exercise by completing the sentence, "If you really knew me, you would know…" He then openly shared how he and his wife were looking at what was next for their family, how he had recently been feeling under the weather, and also how he was concerned that we in the class might misconstrue his excitement about his upcoming course as trying to "sell" us. It was refreshing.

When it was our turn, thanks to some amazing technology, the participants on the call were sectioned off into groups of three and instructed to each take two minutes finishing that sentence: "If you really knew me, you would know..." Just before we were divided into our mini-group, I gulped and thought, "Do I really want to do this?" I wasn't sure I wanted to "expose" myself to strangers. But my fears were immediately allayed when "Allison" from Toronto and "Aaron" from Chicago began speaking.

Allison went first and disclosed that she had been caring for her elderly mother and felt guilty because at times she really didn't want to. Aaron revealed that much of his self-image and value was based on his ability to perform and present well. He shared how much energy it took for him to walk around pretending that he was "perfect." When it was my turn, I admitted that I felt drained from worrying about my sister, who had just lost her job because of her alcoholism. In a matter of minutes, the three of us were connected in a field of support, compassion, and empathy. Through revealing ourselves, we created intimacy.

When someone speaks the truth, it resonates throughout our entire being. Whenever we wholeheartedly share, it creates a palpable connection because we've permitted others to see our true selves. Speaking honestly, when it's from the heart, is also enormously freeing and unifying. Admitting a deep truth aloud to even one person—"I am lonely," "I am sorry," even "I am really gifted in this area"—can rock the truth-teller's world and invite others in. When we speak from our own inner experience, as opposed to throwing around opinions, criticisms, or judgments, we relate and connect.

> **The only way you can experience authentic intimacy and true connection with others is to risk exposing your true self.**
> **—Yvonne and Rich Dutra-St. John**

Speaking Our Selves

There are usually birth pangs to speaking our most authentic self into being. Our ego's tendency to elude the truth, judge, and be "right" can undermine real connection. To speak authentically even at the risk of embarrassment or disapproval requires self-awareness and self-love. Self-awareness helps us recognize when we're in an emotional pinch—when we're triggered and want to lash out or say something to manipulate, punish, or look good. That's our cue to self-soothe our anxiety or fear. By reassuring ourselves that we are loved and valuable, we create a cocoon of emotional safety. Until we're anchored in our own goodness and inherent worth, we'll be less willing to be visible and speak our truth.

Self-love also empowers us to be generous—to be the bigger person. When we remember and affirm that we are inherently "good," we're less likely to be sarcastic, snippy, or hurtful. We find it easier to communicate transparently by "telling on ourselves," sharing what is less than perfect about us, or perhaps being the first one to say "I'm sorry" or "I forgive you" or to acknowledge and appreciate something in the other person. When you speak generously from the heart, you stand taller and brighter.

The Latin root of the word *generous* is *generare*, "to generate." Being generous in our conversations is something *we* bring to the equation. However, it takes practice to generate connection, mutuality, and care in our conversations without abandoning ourselves.

When I first started dating Tom, I was spontaneous, forthright, playful, and flirtatious. As our relationship progressed, I (my ego) became invested in "keeping" him, and I unconsciously started censoring myself. I held back my needs and feelings, tried not to be too "demanding," and made excuses about why he wasn't more attentive. Love wasn't motivating me; it was fear. Even though we were physically intimate, I overrode deeper feelings of discomfort when I was around him. I was uneasy because the real me had been taken hostage by the self-limiting belief that if I said what I was really feeling, he wouldn't love me. I thought that if I let him see my flawed self, he would leave.

When Tom eventually broke it off, I told friends, "He left me." But I actually left him. By withholding my authentic thoughts and feelings, I had all but disappeared: I had abandoned myself. Real intimacy happens only when we share ourselves transparently. When we appear completely "together," we may garner respect and admiration, but not closeness. It's only when we're courageous enough to expose our humanity, flaws and all, that others fall in love with us. When we are willing to express what we think might be unacceptable, there is actually more of us to love.

> **Until we develop the capacity to love and appreciate ourselves just as we are, we will go through life with our noses pressed up against the glass.**
> **—Katherine Woodward Thomas**

Speaking and Listening Generously from the Heart

I'm not recommending "no holds barred" communication. As we've learned in earlier chapters, real connection sometimes requires containing our reactions until we can speak from our more mature and loving self. It helps to ask ourselves about the intent behind our words: Am I communicating to genuinely share, or am I just talking to hear myself? Do I want to relate and connect, or am I attempting to control?

It takes patience and practice, as well, to learn to *listen* generously from the heart. We tend to sort and filter what we hear as it relates to our own cares, concerns, and commitments. Yet as we cultivate self-awareness, we notice when we're listening with a hidden agenda: for where the other person is wrong, for what we agree or disagree with, for how to manipulate the situation to our advantage, or for how we are right. By letting go of this kind of self-interested listening, we remain open to possibility and connection.

Generous listening is giving our undivided attention without judgments, bias, or personal agenda. Katherine Woodward Thomas writes, "Once you have mastered the ability to authentically listen with your whole body, absorbing even the rich subtleties in the unspoken, you will have discovered the key to intimacy. For truly, listening is love in action." To create fulfilling lives and relationships, we also need to become practiced at communicating love. Making this a primary intention inspires us to speak in ways that raise the vibration. This doesn't mean we go around gushing at people. It's also not to be confused with glossing over our real feelings in an attempt to appear "spiritual." Just the opposite—when we speak from the heart, we communicate in ways that honor our feelings and needs while being compassionate to others. We take responsibility to lead the conversation to higher levels of partnership and connection.

Because our words have such a powerful creative impact, when we speak a new possibility for ourselves, we speak our future into being. We lay down the blueprint for what's to come, whether it is to say, "I am committed to creating a loving, intimate relationship," "I will be the outspoken leader I am called to be," "I will no longer tolerate racism," or "I am a sexy, savvy, resourceful woman." What's startling and miraculous about wholehearted speaking is that these heart-felt declarations set into motion an energy that supports the fulfillment of our words.

By learning to enthusiastically speak our joy, gifts, and purpose into the world, we put a stake in the ground for a whole new possibility. What worlds will your heartfelt words create today?

Looking Ahead

Our thoughts ricochet every which way; we can't control them. But we do have dominion over what we choose to say. At this level of the Spiral, you'll not only be inspired to speak in ways that are more transparent and intentional, you will learn how to use the Co-Creative Power of Speech to broaden your vistas and manifest your destiny.

As you gain mastery in using heartfelt words, you will:

- Be inspired to listen and speak in ways that create connection and intimacy
- Learn how to powerfully articulate your value to others
- Unleash energy and joy by practicing authentic transparency
- Learn to speak in ways that bring forth a whole new possibility for your life

Stories

The three stories that follow share a common theme: what becomes possible when we are willing to be scrupulously honest with ourselves before speaking our "truth." When we communicate from a place of rigorous integrity, we give birth to a whole new reality.

Mary's Story: Transform Your Identity

Our success and, even more importantly, our happiness correlate directly with the meaning we make out of what happens to us. This meaning, or the way we interpret life's events, reflects our beliefs and composes our "story."

Mary looked much younger than she was. Her small stature, long blond hair, and button nose didn't always play in her favor at work. Yet, as one coworker said, "Don't let her looks fool you—Mary is a stick of dynamite." Mary's boss, Robin, agreed: "Mary is sharp as a tack, knows her customer base better than anyone, drives things to conclusion, is willing to work hard and dive deep, and knows our products inside and out." But Mary had other qualities as well, which Robin termed a "combative style" and occasional "defeatist attitude," and they threatened to derail Mary's successes. Which is why Robin hired me to work with her.

A few months into our work, Mary told me: "I'm ready to let go of an old story that I'm not smart enough, I'm not good enough, and I'm too junior. Because of these I've been showing up almost aggressively at work. I was overcompensating for what I thought were my failings. I've been pushing people away."

Mary had adopted negative beliefs about herself long ago and had been collecting evidence of them ever since. She decided early on that if she let people see how sensitive she was, they would discount her. Being cool, sarcastic, and blunt was her inept attempt to protect her vulnerability. Now she saw that her negative remarks—her "preemptive strikes"—were causing the exact situation she feared: the perception that she was "junior."

As Mary's defenses softened, she became aware of the tender feelings of her younger self, the part of her that had constructed those limiting beliefs. From the vantage point of her adult self she began to disprove and dismantle them. She could see that in reality she was no longer "junior" in any way. She was a valuable asset to the company and had the respect of others.

Until we register the painful message of what we're telling ourselves, we can't disintegrate the concrete around our old stories. As the light of our consciousness touches these beliefs, they change. Exposing her false beliefs assuaged Mary's fears.

Finally, Mary was ready to make a new declaration: "I am gifted and creative, and people trust and believe in me. I have the heart of a lion." She felt the truth of this deep in her bones. Mary reinforced her new truth by reciting it each morning before work and by looking for evidence of it in her daily interactions. In declaring who she was going to be, Mary was shaping her own destiny. Three months later she was slated for a promotion. Today she is one of the top two women in her company and actively paves the way for other women to rise.

It does pay to be honest. It pays in rewarding relationships. It pays in unblocked energy. It pays in passion. To stand tall in who you are, unafraid to reveal what you want and need, kind enough to tell the truth, and brave

enough to bear the consequences, is a telling sign of spiritual development.

—**Elizabeth Lesser**

Wendy's Story: All-True-Istic Speaking

At a break from a leadership workshop on how to be your most
"generous" self, I called to invite my parents to a special dinner
where I was to receive an award from the National Kidney Foundation in California.

My mom immediately declined. "Wendy, we can't go. You
know that your father was diagnosed with prostate cancer this year."

"But I thought he'd completed his treatment and his doctor
gave him a clean bill of health?"

"Wendy, a cross-country trip would put undue pressure on
him. We just can't do it."

"Mom, this is an important event for me. There are already a
number of tables reserved by friends. I can't believe my own parents won't make the effort!"

We hung up on each other.

This wasn't the first time I felt disappointed by my mother.
During my adolescence, my mother, overwhelmed with five kids
and frustrated with my dad's lack of attention, became depressed
and for a period drank excessively. Although she eventually quit,
I always felt deeply wounded by her neglect. After college, I
moved as far away as I could, to the opposite coast. Over the years
my anger often flared with critical words.

Sensitive to criticism, Mom would become defensive at my
slightest provocation. Deep down, she probably feared that what I
was insinuating was true: that she had failed as a mother and that
she would never measure up to my expectations. True or not, this
deeply grooved pattern kept us at odds.

I returned to the workshop and sat with my familiar resentments. I could feel how far I was from putting into practice what
we were learning about speaking generously. Although what I
had said to her felt true and "right," it left both of us feeling bad.

I was weary from the push-pull dance we had done for more than twenty years. I wanted to move beyond it.

The workshop progressed, and we were led through an exercise on how to discover the truth for ourselves. At any time, our personal truth may differ from what's really going on, and it is always open to interpretation. Our facilitator, Bill Lamond, author of *Born to Lead*, reminded us that the hallmark of truth is that it sets you free. "If you're still struggling with an issue, it's because you haven't gotten to 'The Truth' about it yet," he said. Bill introduced us to three criteria for getting to the heart of any issue:

1.   The truth is always about you, no one else. We often believe that things aren't working because of "them." But we all know how well it works to try and change someone else. Until we "own" our experience, we exist outside the locus of control.

2.   The truth is better than you think, or thought it would be. Because we often take things personally, our mind conjures up all sorts of interpretations that work against us and have no basis in reality.

3.   The truth is something that you have not thought of before. (It made sense that if I had discovered the truth about my issue, it would be a nonissue.)

I was ready to apply the truth inquiry to my stubborn problem. I wrote out: "Regarding my upset with my mother, what is the truth that is only about me, is better than I think, and that I have not thought of before, that, if communicated to myself, will lighten me up and set me free?"

Gloria Steinem's words popped into my mind, "The truth will set you free but first it will piss you off."

I realized that under the guise of being "generous" I had an agenda. On some subterranean level, I was asking my mother to prove that she loved me. Although I could understand and empathize with the angry feelings of my younger self, it struck me how archaic they were. I had no doubt that my mom loved me. She had demonstrated it to me in ways large and small since her lapse long ago. Even more importantly, I had evolved past needing her to be a certain way for me to feel good. I loved me. I was proud of myself and had the love of friends. That definitely felt lighter.

Then I thought, "I want a good relationship with my mother. What is the truth about this that would generate more connection without my abandoning myself?" Another truth bubbled up, not from my younger self's need to be right, but from a place of love and appreciation.

At the next break, I called Mom back and spoke from my heart. "Mom, it's totally okay if you and Dad aren't up for it. Of course I would love to have you there but the truth is I just want you to feel honored too. I wouldn't be getting this award if it weren't for you. You and Dad were there for me when I was sick, and without you I wouldn't be here today. I know that you will be there in spirit and I will be celebrating this award with you."

The best of you is the truth of you. Speaking from my higher self was an expression of the more authentic me, and I felt so much lighter without my old ax to grind. Choosing words that were kinder and more generous, instead of blaming and needy, caused a radical shift: it freed my mother and me from what could have become a lifelong dynamic.

We never went back to it.

Most people's first reaction is usually based on knowledge, data, and facts, but not necessarily on wisdom. The knee-jerk reaction is almost always ego. So you wait and you pray and you listen. And then you might have something wiser to say—something a little more truthful than my little story...

—Richard Rohr

Exercises

As you work with the Co-Creative Power of Feelings in the exercises that follow, you'll find ways to powerfully articulate who you are and the value you provide and speak your truth, even when what you have to say might be unpopular.

Rewrite Your HerStory, Reclaim Your Destiny

The stories we tell ourselves dictate how we live our lives. As we learned from Mary, our limiting beliefs trap us in old stories that don't serve us—or the world. Mary's old story stemmed from a fear-laden belief that she wasn't "enough." Another of my clients, Sarah, was a brilliant economist and former beauty pageant winner. But when I asked about her accomplishments, she said, "I'm not proud of them because they're not mine. I'm living my life as if what matters is what's on the résumé." Sarah's story up till then had been scripted from her lifelong unconscious need to please her parents and live up to their expectations. It hijacked her true destiny and also exempted her from going for something that she really wanted.

The Untrue Story: Identify the story you've been living until now. We'll call it your "Untrue Story." This may be the story of your defeats, your fears, your limitations. Who is the protagonist in that story (clue—she's often our "victim" self)? Give her a name. Mary's name was "Junior Mary." "Helga" was the name that Sarah used to epitomize her martyred, obedient, overly responsible self. My own wimpy protagonist calls herself "Wendy Whiner," but don't tell anyone!

Your True Story: Now it's time to create your "True Story" based on the power, beauty, and magnificence of who you really are. Consider all that you have gone through to become who you are today. From this perspective we each have a "shero" within. Owning up to the truth of herself, Mary called forth her shero in the name "Mary, the Lionhearted." Another client, Linda, tapped into her confident, sassy self with her shero name, "Lolita." Sarah called her bright, energized, bold self into being with "Ms. Vivacity." Naming her inner shero gave voice to her soul's desire to spend more time riding her beloved horse, being creative, and saying no to what she didn't want. Now it's your turn: What will you name yourself?

Naming your "shero" anchors you in the new story you are creating for your life. Your shero name is a reminder of the truth of who you are and will pull you into your desired destiny. So name her, claim her. And start living your new story today.

You cannot enter any world for which you do not have a language.

—David Whyte

Self-Advocacy: Craft a Shining Example

Would you like to be able to speak more powerfully about your talents and gifts? Being able to tell short, vivid success stories that leave a positive and memorable impression is an essential career skill. The following exercise serves a dual purpose: it offers you a step-by-step architecture for articulating how your gifts create value for others and it builds self-esteem.

As you compose anecdotes about how you have demonstrated skills, abilities, or strengths, you'll gain confidence in the unique and valuable ways that you contribute to the world. And by creating a collection of these success stories, or shining examples, you'll be better prepared to showcase your talents and take advantage of opportunities as they present themselves.

To start, determine what you are passionate about and what qualities you want to emphasize. Then select incidents (paid or volunteer) that best highlight those. Make a list of up to three examples that best exemplify your gifts and accomplishments. Examples: grooming two people on my team to be world class, bringing lightness and humor to a tense business meeting, speaking from the heart in ways that challenged the status quo.

Now select one of your work or volunteer experiences and complete the following four steps to transform it into a Shining Example.

1. **The introduction: set up your skills.** Describe your strength or set of skills to the interested party and ask, "May I give you an example of how I've used that?" For instance, "cleaning up an oil spill" might draw upon your skills of inspiring collaboration and teamwork and creating order out of chaos. Examples of skill: attention to detail, achieving market growth, building strong relationships.

2. **The opportunity: what was the situation that called for your gifts?** Was there a crisis? A problem? An unmet need? How did it get to be your problem? Why was it important to meet the need? What was at stake for the individual or company? Was there a risk involved? Examples of opportunities: the company was downsizing, my team was global so I had to improve communications, I wanted to help a friend.

3. **Action taken: what did you do?** How did you do it? What knowledge, abilities, skills, or assets did you access? Point out any credential, experience,

or core competency that you drew upon. Don't get caught up in the mental logjam of "I don't want to overstate what I do." Let yourself really shine here. Examples: I practiced my pitch until I knew it by heart, I brought all key management to the table and surfaced key assumptions about the business, I kicked off a campaign for managers to share their success stories at every meeting.

4. Noticeable outcome: how did you make a difference? What were the quantifiable results? Sum up the story with concrete outcomes (using numbers where appropriate).

Examples: We beat the competition by a 10 percent margin, we won the top award, we reduced carbon dioxide emissions by 20 percent. Where relevant, also mention personal rewards (praise, a promotion, an award, gratification). Examples: I won the Best Salesperson Award, I received a promotion, I surpassed my quotas and received a bonus.

Shining examples can be used when interviewing for a new opportunity or just to help others see your potential. Repeat this process for two more shining examples. Then create abridged versions of your stories and proudly tell them wherever and whenever appropriate.

> **What would happen if one woman told the truth about her life? The world would split open.**
> **—Muriel Rukeyser**

Speak Truth to Power

It takes courage to speak the truth in situations where we may feel outnumbered or outranked. Our patriarchal culture has a tendency to punish the truth teller, and as women we can find ourselves ostracized if we speak out or blow the whistle, so we often remain silent when we long to tell it like we see it. And yet, when we learn to speak truth to power we don't just regain a vital sense of self-worth and empowerment, we also begin to shift the dominant culture in positive and sometimes radical ways. Here's how you can speak your truth while staying calm, collected, and connected.

Set your intention: Get clear about your desired outcome.

Know your motivation: Make sure your words come from a place of service, not self-aggrandizement.

Use your head: Back up what you have to say with facts, statistics, and research. This will give your words gravitas and have people take you seriously.

Trust your heart: Once you have your intentions, motivations, and facts down, you can trust yourself to speak from your heart.

What is it that you long to say? Spend a few moments writing down some of the truths that you are longing to speak right now.

> Most people speak without intention; they simply say whatever comes to mind. Speak with intention, and your actions take on new purpose. Speak with power, and you act with power.
>
> —Fernando Flores

Highlights

- When we generously allow others a glimpse into who we really are, we create intimacy and connectedness.
- Revealing our inner experience in the moment is qualitatively different from stating an opinion or judgment.
- Self-love supports us in speaking from a place of vulnerability.
- We can generate self-love anytime by reassuring ourselves that we are loved, inherently "good," and valuable.
- Sharing our success stories is an essential part of owning our power.
- It's natural to feel fear when we speak truth to power, just don't let it stop you.
- Because our words have such a powerful creative impact, when we speak a new possibility for ourselves, we speak our future into existence.

CHAPTER 17

You Can Save and Savor the World

The Co-Creative Power of Action

I wake up each morning torn between a desire to save the world and a desire to savor the world. This makes it very hard to plan the day.

—E. B. White

I applaud your success! When you embarked on the transformative journey of the Spiral, you didn't really know what you would find. By now, you have discovered more of the real you and the freedom to live by your deepest knowing. You are in the process of reclaiming the feminine qualities of care, relatedness, and well-being not just for yourself and your family, but for the larger community. You have had aha moments and you have acted upon them to change your life for the better. You have evolved yourself, and you are probably eager to continue opening to more freedom, love, and joy. And you will.

At this level of the Spiral, in our passion to live an inspired life, we return one last time to the Co-Creative Power of Action. As you've learned so far, action becomes a Co-Creative Power when we act from our highest ideals and soul desires, regardless of inner or outer resistance. We take the hand of our worries or fears and walk steadily toward what brings us alive. We do the inner work to evolve the parts of ourselves that make us want to play small. We show up in new ways for others and the world, anchored in the greater truth of who we are and who we can become.

The implications here are profound. Our inner work opens the way for inspired actions in the world around us. As we evolve from the ego's priorities for comfort, security, and success for success's sake, what gets revealed is our deeper imperative to birth our unique gifts to make a contribution to the greater good.

So many of us are waking up to our higher potentials at this time. As we come alive to our gifts and flourish in unprecedented ways, we sense that our impulse to self-actualize is not just personal. We live on the cusp of deep reckonings; so much at stake in the larger world calls us to rise to our full power. And women, arguably, are hearing the loudest call. As Archbishop Desmond Tutu wrote, "Our earth home and all forms of life in it are at grave risk. We men have had our turn and made a proper mess of things. We need women to save us."

Archbishop Tutu's words can feel like a tall order, asking more than we may want to give. Giving of ourselves, though, is not about self-sacrifice. E. B. White wrote wryly of being "torn between a desire to save the world and a desire to savor the world"—but the truth is we don't have to choose. This is what the Co-Creative Power of Action teaches us: our happiness and the world's needs are sacredly linked.

Happiness in Action

The ultimate outcome of all goals is happiness. Everything we want, we want because we think it will make us feel better. So before we take action on this Third Turning of the Spiral, let's take a closer look at the origins of happiness.

One of the earliest seminal works on happiness was written by the former president of the American Psychological Association, Martin Seligman, who took on this inquiry: "What are the enabling conditions that make human beings flourish?" His book, *Authentic Happiness*, defined three types of happiness: (1) pleasure (sensory and bodily pleasures, fun, entertainment, and excitement); (2) engagement (our depth of involvement in work, relationships, communities, and hobbies); and (3) meaning (using personal strengths to some larger end).

Western culture encourages us to build lives around the pursuit of pleasure. The trouble is, if we're always in pursuit we're not really savoring life. Experiencing pleasure, however ephemeral, is one of the joys of being human, but as Seligman points out, it is the least consequential path to fulfillment. Our level of engagement with life and the degree to which we utilize our innate virtues and strengths are far greater determinants of our happiness or well-being.

Recall what you learned in the First Turning about your inner "daimon," your wisest golden self. Brain researchers from the University of

Wisconsin–Madison report that one of the most enduring components of overall wellbeing is *eudaimonia*. Composed from the Greek *eu* ("good") and *daimon* ("spirit" or "deity"), eudaimonia means striving toward excellence based on one's unique talents and potential. This is the magical combination of "engagement" and "meaning." Women who take on new challenges aligned with their sense of purpose benefit immensely, both psychologically and physically. They experience the sweet spot of success, the marriage of achievement and actualization. Richie J. Davidson, PhD, points out, "Eudaimonic wellbeing is much more robust and satisfying than hedonic happiness."

According to leading researchers in the field of positive psychology who discovered the Happiness Formula, there are a number of factors that contribute to our happiness, from our genetic "set point" (which can be raised through meditation and certain kinds of therapy) to our conditions of living (something most of us expend a good deal of energy trying to improve even though they only affect our happiness by a mere 7 to 10 percent). For instance: a better body, the "right" spouse, more money, a nicer home, and so on.

Here is why the Co-Creative Power of Action is so important. Scientists found that a full 40 percent of our happiness comes from voluntary intentional activity: anything we do consistently and on purpose. This activity is further divided into two categories: actions that are "self" oriented and actions that are "other" oriented. If our actions are for personal pleasure, they produce momentary, transient happiness. On the other hand, actions that serve others are a surefire way to produce deep and lasting fulfillment. The conclusion: the quickest and most assured route to happiness is to find ways to use your gifts to advance the greater good.

The specifics of *how* you work to help others hardly matter. What is important is taking steps toward what calls to you—even if it scares you. Remember, the universe loves bravery. When we're inspired to act as an agent of change on behalf of something that really matters, our own reservations and fears fade. When we accomplish something we didn't think we could, we become emboldened to act even more courageously.

To put it another way, we find our courage when we find our calling. Arianna Huffington makes this case in her book *On Becoming Fearless*. She tells the story of Rory Kennedy, who made a film about the global AIDS crisis and found that she could put her own fears of public speaking aside when advocating for people whose voices are rarely heard. She only had to think of Leck, her friend who died of AIDS, to put aside all her reservations and act from her heart.

And did you know that this kind of heartfelt courage is catching? Psychology professor Jonathan Haidt, PhD (aptly pronounced like "height"), uses the word "Elevation" to describe what we feel when we witness what he calls moral beauty. "Elevation seems to have a ripple effect, triggering cognitive, emotional, and behavioral changes," Haidt says. "It makes people more open, more loving, grateful, compassionate and forgiving." In one study, people who watched a documentary of Mother Teresa tending to orphans felt more loving afterward and were more likely to volunteer for charitable work than a group that viewed clips from *America's Funniest Home Videos*. Seeing—or even just reading or hearing about—others' generosity, bravery, and kindness not only makes us happier and healthier (by boosting our immune systems); it also increases the likelihood that we'll help others. And every time we "pay it forward" we contribute to the upward spiral of good. In Arianna Huffington's words, "The moment we begin to change, the world starts changing with us because we are all interconnected."

A Time to Give

There has never been a time when we have felt our interconnectedness more. Technology has enabled us to see and feel each other's joys and pain and spurred us to take up our role as global citizens. Our experience of interconnectedness becomes real to us through acts of giving and receiving. There is a synergistic relationship between the two. Based on what we've learned about its psychological and physiological benefits, giving *is* receiving: acts of generosity show a scientific correlation with pain relief, stronger hearts, immune function, and overall resilience. As psychiatrist Karl Menninger observed, "Love cures people. Both the ones who give it and the ones who receive it."

If your giving is not inherently paying you back, an adjustment may be in order. Are you slowing down to savor your life? Are you an over-giver? Perhaps you are giving from a place of lack?

We don't need to be scientists in a lab measuring brain activity to know if we're giving from fullness, untainted by the need to please, to feel appreciated, or to fix someone. There is a simple elegance to this Third Turning of Action—and it's beautifully stated here by spiritual teacher Nataji: "If your giving is not making you more whole, then you're not giving from a clean place." The capacity to deeply care is a fundamental feminine trait but it has to start with our own self-nurturing.

What may surprise you, however, is the grace and power you'll embody when you find your "right work." It is the universe's way of telling you that you've hit the mother lode.

What is yours to give? What really inspires you, excites you? What is your deepest desire to create, contribute, and experience? What are you good at that can help people in ways large and small?

It's time to step up and give the fullness of your gifts. If they are yours they are magnificent. In the giving of them you will realize your wholeness and so will the world. Eve Ensler says, "When we give in the world what we want the most, we heal the broken part inside each of us."

> **Your living large—your being your true self despite fear, fatigue, doubt, and opposition—will serve the world more than you can imagine. In fact, it may help save it. And saving the world, after all, is what all heroes (including you) are here to do.**
>
> **—Martha Beck**

Looking Ahead

Working with the Co-Creative Power of Action in this final chapter, you will hone in on your "true gifts" and plug into the reenergizing and self-reinforcing cycle of heartfelt giving and receiving.

As you find your own ways to save and savor the world, you will:

- Discover your passion to make a difference and the unwavering belief that you can
- Unearth important clues to finding your true gifts and calling
- Discover your "stand" so that life becomes more expansive and meaningful
- Be inspired to share your gifts in a way that creates connection
- Learn how to keep your upward spiral flowing forever

> **Human generosity is possible because at the center of the solar system a magnificent stellar generosity pours forth free energy . . . without the slightest hesitation. This is the way of the Universe. . . . We have an impulse inside to give.**
>
> **—Brian Swimme**

Stories

Whether they involve big actions or small ones, the following stories show that life becomes richer and more meaningful when it is organized around something larger than yourself—and in the process, you may just find you have helped to make the world a better place.

Wendy's Story: What Is Yours to Do?

I might have never really known my nephew, Chase, if it had been up to his mom. Sheila was scared of the world and kept everything under latch and key. I made an effort to stay close to my sister even though we were on different coasts, and when Chase was four I went to Atlanta to visit them for Christmas. Although I had met him as a baby, this time we recognized each other as long lost playmates. He used to climb up on me—all of his three-foot self—and lay his body on top of mine for closeness. I taught him to ride a bike, helped him build his first snowman, and introduced him to surfing. Sheila adored her son but she was a world-class worrier, and her coping ability grew steadily worse as she began drinking heavily. One day she left Chase in the car while she went into a bar. She lost custody of her son to the State of Georgia, and he was temporarily placed in a nearby foster home where she could still see him. Somewhere deep down I thought it might come to the point where he needed to come live with me, and I applied to a hard-to-get-into Waldorf School minutes from where I live.

The courts told us that if a family member didn't take Chase, he would be put up for adoption. So that he could remain close to his mother, Chase went to live with another sister nearby. But after some time it wasn't working out and she asked me for help—would I take him? That same week he was visiting me in California. We had rented a cottage on the beach so he could take surf lessons. I was walking back from the beach when my phone rang. It was the principal of the school that I had applied to four years before, but that had never had any room, saying that Chase had won the lottery draw for the one opening in his grade.

I had known deep down that raising Chase was mine to do but I was afraid to say yes. Never had I made anyone more important than myself. I wanted to finish writing this book, I had never raised a child, and I hadn't even really fully shared my life with anyone, let alone put someone else first. I knew Chase would have emotional baggage—could I handle it? And I knew that if I took him on there was no going back. He had already experienced enough abandonment. It was a serious commitment. Taking care of him would disrupt my plan, my schedule, my sleep, and even, at times, my ability to do my work. And yet, what I discovered was that this was the answer to something that I craved. The truth was I wanted a less hygienic life, a messy life with laughter and family, the whole rough and tumble of it. I was scared, but when I thought about my life from the end of my life—the happy, wise older me looking back on this choice—I knew I had to say yes. That same week, another drinking binge took his mother's life.

The universe is always telling us—pointing us—in the right direction. We need to be open and accepting, to listen to the signs and then to engage rather than waiting for something to happen. If I had never followed my heart's impulse to insert myself into this young boy's life, I might never have been blessed with this larger life. By acting on my deeper knowing, my life—and Chase's—has changed for the better.

Just do right. Right may not be expedient; it may not be profitable, but it will satisfy your soul.

—Maya Angelou

Our Stories: Women's Evolutionary Leadership Conferences

For the past three years, I've been hosting women's conferences in Silicon Valley that bring together top female corporate leaders with other professional women who crave authentic connection.

The rich, interactive dialogues between the speakers and audience always get to the heart of what women want: to step into the most authentic, powerful version of themselves and change the world for the better.

A central part of what makes these events unique is the way they come together. I'm joined by a group of amazing volunteers who, like beautiful notes of music, combine their skills to create a stirring symphony. These women bring their production prowess, organization skills, and event planning expertise in order to create something truly special. We all know why we're a part of the team: we are marshaling our talents to help women rise in every way—in politics, in organizations, and in creative self-expression.

I'm frequently asked, "How do you create so much intimacy in a room full of Silicon Valley professional women?" It's because, from the first interaction, everything we do and communicate is in service of deeper connection. Each woman on the team, and all those we come in contact with, feel heard, acknowledged, and appreciated. This foundation of deep connection creates magic that plays out in every event.

At our *Women As Catalysts of Change* event the panelists shared how they became leaders—the good, the bad, and the ugly. They exhibited such an honest level of disclosure that the experience of authentic leadership became accessible to every woman in the room. At another event, Tiffany Shlain, honored by *Newsweek* as one of the "Women Shaping the 21st Century," arrived in polka-dot high heels and a jaunty hat. An author, award-winning filmmaker, and speaker, she could have just gone through the motions and we would have loved her anyway. Instead, she connected with us through her vulnerability, sharing the roller-coaster ride of her creative process—the hard times as well as the good ones. Through her authentic presence, she created a circle of intimacy that played out in the small group conversations that followed.

When we are truly giving our gifts, we connect with ourselves, the quirky, vulnerable and sometimes less-than-perfect beings that we are. And we aren't afraid of anyone seeing us or knowing us, because we are refueled by the experience of knowing another and being known. I've seen women making presentations search for their reading glasses, lose their notes, and even, very occasionally, the thread of their talk. But the thread of connection—the one that runs between them and the women listening to them—always stays strong. They're willing to be afraid, to be genuine, to be imperfect, in service of not only getting their message out but also in creating an enlightening and uplifting experience for the audience. Our motto is "Connection, not perfection!"

When we show up in this unabashedly real way, we are already change makers. I have seen women in the audience who arrived feeling deeply alone, leave feeling a part of something warm, generative, and inspiring. No longer isolated, they feel empowered to go back into their lives just a little bit stronger, a little bit wiser, and even more committed to unleashing their voice, their aspirations, and their power into the world.

Exercises

In our hyper-masculine culture we tend to adopt an assertive, make-it-happen approach to try to figure out and pursue "right livelihood." But trying to control the precise way in which our gifts and passions find their outlet in the world isn't our job. In the Spiral journey it's much more efficient (and fun) to call on our feminine, magnetic strengths.

Our primary job, then, becomes stoking the fire of our passions and getting to know ourselves from the inside out: our values, our strengths, what calls to us, and whom we love to serve. As we come to know these elements, our "offer" comes into focus, and our gifts match up with an unmet need in the form of an opportunity—kismet happens. This grace-filled union of purpose, passion, and need is available to everyone. What you love to do, some person or organization is crying out for. As we get clearer and more fired up about what we have to give, it's like our signal gets louder and louder until finally the universe "hears" us—and responds with surprising opportunities. Often right in our own backyard!

The following exercises are designed to crystallize your combination of passions and talents to turn up the volume on your signal to the universe.

Finding Your True Gifts

As Thich Nhat Hanh taught, we each have "near gifts" and "true gifts." We find our calling at the place where our true gifts intersect with others' needs and the needs of the world. The following questions will help you identify your true gifts and discover your calling—the inspired action that the world needs from you now. The questions may seem similar, but I suggest you answer them all; they're designed to help you discover themes in your answers.

What valuable "gifts" or ways of relating do you bring to a variety of situations (home, work, with friends)? Examples: seeing the underlying issue, getting something started, telling the truth.

What can you do best that would make the world a better place for yourself and others? Examples: create a warm and inviting home, support those I believe in, be a role model to children.

What are you doing when you feel "in the flow"? Examples: working with numbers, coaching others, networking.

Now that you know your gifts, strengths, and what puts you in the flow—who could use them? Imagine that you are serving others while also serving your soul's calling. From the eyes of your evolutionary self, what do you imagine? When you daydream, what do you see yourself doing? Examples: working with a small team, working with animals, cultivating my spiritual side.

List at least five ideas for your "calling."

Letter to a Change Maker

Whether you know it or not, you are probably already a change maker. As you consider the ways you positively influence others, imagine the letter you would like to receive from an individual, group, or organization that you have helped. For instance, if you enabled a child to go to college, what might he say to you about what that has meant to him? I received the following letter from a woman in Afghanistan who has been helped by my sponsorship. It brought me to tears of gratitude to be in a position to make a difference to a woman whose life was so different from my own, and yet who is in many ways a "sister."

> My beloved sister Wendy Wallbridge
> Thank you very much for the way that you have chosen me without knowing me and that you have agreed to sponsor me in this program of Women for Women. I am very happy that your sponsorship is helping me to improve to a better life.
> I am married and I have a husband and three children. They are all doing well. I am 50 years old. I am using the sponsorship to buy some hens and a pig
> I am concluding here thank you very much and bless you
> your sister
> Margaret (Mukamana Maligarito)

Now it's your turn: Write the letter to yourself, staying open to the difference that you can make in the world.

We build up our moral muscle by exercising it. We become virtuous by the practice of virtue, responsible by the practice of responsibility, generous by the practice of generosity and compassionate by the practice of compassion.

—Arianna Huffington

Give What You Want the Most

Two midwives were attending a birth, and the mother-to-be had been in labor for hours. She was working very hard, with everyone, including her husband, doing their best to support her. At one point the labor just froze. Dilation stopped and nothing was happening. Exhausted, she looked to the midwives for help. Almost out of options to offer, one of them suggested that the mom-to-be rub her tired husband's shoulders. She looked up at the midwife in complete disbelief. "What do you mean, he's tired? I'm the one laboring!"

But when she looked over and saw her husband, she saw the man that she loved, wide-eyed and shaken, his T-shirt wet with perspiration. She reached over, pulled him close and began stroking his back. After just a few minutes, her labor kicked back in. By taking her attention off herself and nurturing her beloved with the love and tenderness that she most needed, everything began to flow.

Make a list of what you want the most: love, affection, tenderness, kindness, prosperity, attention, time, friendships, appreciation. Then make it a point to give that to someone else this week.

What's Your Stand?

When I was fifteen my best friend, Karen, and I got our parents' permission to attend an outdoor concert (chaperoned by her older brothers) in a town a few hours away. All that we knew about it was that there would be some great bands. It turned out to be Woodstock. Being at Woodstock was like falling through Alice's rabbit hole into an entirely different world. The three days of freedom, cooperation, and generosity of spirit (not to mention the mud) lit a possibility in me for a new way of living that was openhearted and free. It set me on a quest to find higher levels of love and freedom in myself and in the world.

Today that commitment to freedom shows up in the way I coach executives (and my adopted son) to be fully self-expressed. I also express it through the "stand" I take for women to step into their purpose and power in full partnership with men. When you find out what you really believe in—what your life is about—and make a stand for it, your life unfolds. Knowing my "stand" gives me direction and helps me prioritize.

A stand isn't about being right, being better, or taking any contrary position. It isn't something we make up but rather something we declare by knowing what we care deeply about. A stand is always bigger than our own self-interests—it is an ideal that we might even be willing to die for. It's also something that never tires or gets old—it's so big that it can't get accomplished in one lifetime. There's always more freedom, more self-expression, more self-liberation to be accessed. And when we put a stake in the ground for something that has real meaning to us, it compels us to act. Without that we can be tentative, paralyzed even—finding it difficult to get past "I don't want to." But when we have a larger context for what we're doing, any pettiness or grumpiness disappears. You recognize that you're an instrument larger than your own agenda and you can do whatever it takes in the name of your calling.

When we are in the presence of our own stand or someone else who has taken a powerful stand in life, like Nelson Mandela, Julia Butterfly Hill, or Martin Luther King Jr., they are irresistible and their enthusiasm contagious.

To discover your stand, ask yourself:

What moves you? What are you attracted to?
What have you longed for?
Who are some of your greatest heroes?
What do you feel passionately about?
What cause or issue stirs you up?
What disturbs you about the way our world is?
Why are you drawn to what you are doing? Why that client? Why that
    company?
What do you stand for?

Examples of stands: for every child to have the opportunity for a healthy and productive life, for every human being to have access to beauty—her own and in the world—the full equality of women.

It doesn't have to be grandiose. Yours might be as simple as a stand for a wonderful life for yourself, your family, your friends and all people, or a stand for the women in your company.

Give me a place to stand and I will move the world.
—Archimedes

Highlights

- As we evolve, we naturally find ways to use our true gifts to make a contribution to the greater good.
- When our masculine strengths of focus, strategy, and action work in service to our feminine gifts of love, care, and relatedness, we can help cure society's ills.
- Striving for something significant, whether it's developing a talent or raising resilient children, gives us meaning and helps us thrive.
- When that activity is oriented toward helping others or the world, it produces deep fulfillment and a sense of lasting happiness.
- To develop our "true gifts" we often have to say no to giving our "near gifts."
- Life becomes more meaningful when it is organized around something larger than ourselves.

It's not just about hope and ideas, its about action...our
duty is to have a dream but work everyday for reality.
—Shirin Ebadi, Nobel Prize winner

SPIRAL ON

In a TEDx talk given by global activist Lynne Twist, she shared a prescient Native American prophecy that says that the twenty-first century is the time when the Bird of Humanity stops relying solely on one wing to fly. The male wing has gotten incredibly muscular flapping almost violently as the bird circles round and round struggling to keep the Bird of Humanity aloft. The other wing, the female wing, has been limp, weak, and not fully extended. But, as the prophecy foretells, when the female wing fully expresses itself, fully extends—the male wing can relax and the Bird of Humanity can soar. It can Spiral Up!

Your newly claimed powers and your ability to put the muscle of your masculine strengths in service to your feminine wisdom are critically needed today. Not just for your own happiness, fulfillment, and wholehearted success, but for the world's. The integration of your masculine and feminine— your ability to be both generative and receptive—supports you in taking bold actions and making choices consistent with your vision. It also helps you to discern when to suspend the impulse to act and allow the universe's intelligence and timing to lead. In this process you have learned not to force your will upon the universe but to be receptive to what wants to be born through you. When you allow life to unfold, patterns emerge from seeming randomness and you are led to the next rung on your Spiral. Life is inviting you to expand and express at a deeper level all the time. Where are you being asked to step up to leadership? Where are you being invited to shift a conversation? Where is your voice needed? You don't need to know your ultimate destination, simply the next right thing.

As we come to the end of our journey together, a new era begins for you. You join the throngs of women who have spread their wings by calling on their Co-Creative Powers to live a more authentic, turned-on life. They have created new opportunities, gotten promotions, slowed down, stepped up, fallen in love, and deeply transformed themselves while shifting the trajectory of their lives. Like them, you have not just evolved, you have awakened to the possibility of life at a new level. And the incredible thing about waking up is that once you wake up, you can never go back to sleep. You now know the difference between living life by default and the exhilaration of a consciously co-created life. Anything but that will pale in comparison.

That doesn't mean that you will always be elevated. We need both descents and ascents to continue to grow and transform on the evolutionary path of becoming our truest selves. There may be times when you find yourself in the bottom loop, feeling as if you have regressed. You haven't! There is never a wrong place to be. Even the plateaus—those times when nothing new seems to be happening—are there to help you assimilate experiences and incubate new creations. Every experience in your Spiral journey is an exciting new opportunity to be more transparent, more honest, more loving, and bolder in expressing yourself in the world.

When I finally committed to turning my ideas into a book that could reach a wider audience of women, I took a miniature blank journal and created a beautiful cover with the title *Spiraling Upward*. I took it down to the creek that runs by my house and dug a small hole, planting it in the dry riverbed. Today, you hold the blossom from that seed in your hands.

My hope for this book is that it will allow what's inside you to be born through you. Just as I believed in my book before it was visible, I believe that any dream you hold can find full expression. I may not know you, but I carry you in my heart and in my dreams of what the future can be when women arise and fulfill their magnificent potential. As you continue to evolve, I know you will reveal more and more of your authentic self and true gifts, and the beauty of who you are will light up the world.

Together we are rising.

ACKNOWLEDGMENTS

This book would never have come to fruition had it not been for my scholarly friend, cowriter, boot-in-the butt coach, and brilliant editor, author Mary Reynolds Thompson. When the ideas for this book were taking shape I prayed to find a writing partner. I had been working solo for three years but it was only when Mary, whom I had gotten to know through our writing group and who lived just up the hill, agreed to work with me that the process actually became fun. We laughed, cried, railed, and danced this book into existence together. Thank you to my longtime friends and allies, the visionary entrepreneurs Bettina and Mike Jetter, whose belief in me and the Spiral Up process strengthened my resolve to write this book.

It is impossible to fully acknowledge all of the amazing authors and spiritual teachers who contributed to my transformative process over the last three decades and who influenced the ideas in my book. You will notice the echo of their voices in my words and recognize their names from the quotations peppered throughout.

Deep love and appreciation goes to my friends and participants in the Spiral Up! Leading with Power & Grace course who pestered me relentlessly to write a book as well as to those who generously allowed me to share their personal stories: Stacie S., Peggy B., Linda L., Mary A., Lynn K., Tina C., Susan P., Jill E., Tyra J., Lynne T., Lisa B., and Randy M., as well as all the wonderful women who chose to remain anonymous.

And last but not least, a deep bow to my family, and to my dear friends: Randy Roberts, Susan Greene, Betsy McKinney, Delisa Sage, and Maryann Molinari, who both cheered me on and put up with my absence.

NOTES

Chapter 1

Page 1: Catalyst, "Statistical Overview of Women in the Workplace," March 3, 2014, http://www.catalyst.org/knowledge/statistical-overview-women-workplace; Bureau of Labor Statistics, Current Population Survey, "Table 11: Employed Persons by Detailed Occupation, Sex, Race, and Hispanic or Latino Ethnicity," *Annual Averages 2012* (2013), http://www.bls.gov/cps/cpsaat11.htm.

Chapter 5

Page 44: Institute of Heart Math, "Science of The Heart: Exploring the Role of the Heart in Human Performance, An Overview of Research Conducted by the Institute of HeartMath," http://www.heartmath.org/research/science-of-the-heart/head-heart-interactions.html?submenuheader=3.

Page 45: John Gerzema, *The Athena Doctrine: How Women (and the Men Who Think Like Them) Will Rule the Future* (San Francisco: Jossey-Bass, 2013), http://www.johngerzema.com/books/athena-doctrine.

Page 47: Coleman Barks, trans., *The Essential Rumi* (New York: HarperCollins, 1995). Used by permission.

Page 48: Glenn Close, interviewed by Oprah Winfrey, *The Oprah Winfrey Show,* May 15, 2009. Also see http://www.cnn.com/2009/LIVING/wayoflife/06/19/o.puppies.behind.bars/index.html?eref=time_us. Also see National Geographic, http://channel.nationalgeographic.com/wild/videos/puppies-behind-bars/.

Page 49: Judith Orloff, *Emotional Freedom: Liberate Yourself from Negative Emotions and Transform Your Life* (New York: Harmony/Random House, 2009).

Chapter 6

Page 58: Bruce Lipton, *Spontaneous Evolution: Our Positive Future (And a Way to Get There from Here)* (Carlsbad, CA: Hay House, 2009).

Page 60: Thich Nhat Hanh, *Fear: Essential Wisdom for Getting Through the Storm* (New York: HarperCollins, 2012).

Page 62: Caroline Casey, *The Visionary Activist*, KPFA, http://coyotenetworknews.com/radio-show/.

Page 63: Max Brockman, ed., *What's Next? Dispatches on the Future of Science: Original Essays from a New Generation of Scientists* (New York: Vintage/Random House, 2009).

Page 63: Julia Cameron, *The Artist's Way: A Spiritual Path to Higher Creativity* (New York: Penguin Putnam, 1992).

Chapter 7

Page 73: Peter Senge, C. Otto Scharmer, Joseph Jaworski, and Betty Sue Flowers, *Presence: Human Purpose and the Field of the Future* (New York: Doubleday, 2004).

Chapter 9

Page 98: Byron Katie, *Who Would You Be Without Your Story? Dialogues with Byron Katie* (Carlsbad, CA: Hay House, 2008).

Page 101: Matthew A. Killingsworth and Daniel T. Gilbert, "A Wandering Mind Is an Unhappy Mind," *Science* 330, no. 932 (November 12, 2010), DOI: 10.1126/science.1192439.

Page 109: Peter Senge, C. Otto Scharmer, Joseph Jaworski, and Betty Sue Flowers, *Presence: Human Purpose and the Field of the Future* (New York: Doubleday, 2004).

Chapter 10

Page 111: Rainer Maria Rilke, *Rilke's Book of Hours: Love Poems to God*, trans. Joanna Macy (New York: Riverhead Books, 1996). Used by permission.

Page 112: Krista Tippett, "The Soul Checkup," *O, The Oprah Magazine,* May 2007: 111–112.

Page 112: From Charlie Rose's interview with Dustin Hoffman, originally aired May 3, 1999.

Chapter 11

Page 123: "Women's Liberation Revisited" *Time*, March 20, 1972: 30–31.

Page 124: Eve Ensler, *I Am an Emotional Creature: The Secret Life of Girls Around the World* (New York: Random House, 2010).

Page 124: Jane Fonda, *My Life So Far* (New York: Random House, 2005).

Page 125: Jane Fonda, *My Life So Far* (New York: Random House, 2005).

Page 125: Jennifer Openshaw, *The Millionaire Zone: Seven Winning Steps to a Seven-Figure Fortune* (New York: Hyperion, 2007).

Page 130: *O, The Oprah Magazine,* "The Power of Loud: Anna Deavere Smith," from "O's First-Ever Power List: 20 remarkable visionaries who are flexing their muscles in business and finance, politics and justice, science and the arts," http://www.oprah.com/money/Power-Women-O-The-Oprah-Magazines-Power-List#ixzz3JqovDm8q.

Chapter 12

Page 137: Jim Stovall, *The Ultimate Gift* (Colorado Springs, CO: David C. Cook, 2001).

Page 138: Caroline Myss, interviewed by Oprah Winfrey, *Super Soul Sunday,* June 24, 2012. Also see, Oprah Winfrey, "Caroline Myss' Advice for Getting to the Heart of Who You Are," *O, The Oprah Magazine*, January, 2013.

Page 138: Agnes De Mille, *Martha: The Life and Work of Martha Graham* (New York: Random House, 1991): 264.

Page 144: W. H. Murray, *The Scottish Himalayan Expedition* (London: J.M. Dent, 1951).

Chapter 13

Page 162: Taken from "Excerpts from the Seminar held at the Foundation for A Course in Miracles, Temecula, California, Kenneth Wapnick, PhD," http://www.facim.org/online-learning-aids/excerpt-series/the-inner-voice/part-ii.aspx.

Page 163: Coleman Barks, trans., *The Soul of Rumi: A New Collection of Ecstatic Poems* (New York: HarperCollins, 2002). Used by permission.

Page 164: Wendy Palmer, *The Intuitive Body: Discovering the Wisdom of Conscious Embodiment and Aikido* (Berkeley, CA: Blue Snake Books/North Atlantic, 2008).

Chapter 14

Page 165: Daniel Pink, *A Whole New Mind: Why Right-Brainers Will Rule the Future* (London: Penguin, 2006): 1.

Page 166: Katherine Russell Rich, "In a Single Stroke: The Metamorphosis of Jill Bolte Taylor," *O, The Oprah Magazine*, October 2002.

Page 166: Katherine Russell Rich, "In a Single Stroke: The Metamorphosis of Jill Bolte Taylor," *O, The Oprah Magazine*, October 2002.

Page 175: Mary Manin Morrissey, *Building Your Field of Dreams* (New York: Bantam: 1997).

Chapter 15

Page 177: Deepak Chopra, interviewed on *The Ellen DeGeneres Show*, October 27, 2009.

Page 178: Jessica Winter, "What Really Makes People Happy." *O, The Oprah Magazine,* May 2009: 166–171.

Page 178: Stephen Buhner, *Sacred Plant Medicine: The Wisdom in Native American Herbalism* (Rochester, VT: Inner Traditions, 2006): xxi.

Page 179: Robert Holden, *Happiness Now! Timeless Wisdom for Feeling Good FAST* (Carlsbad, CA: Hay House, 2007).

Page 179: Richard Davidson and Antoine Lutz, "Buddha's Brain: Neuroplasticity and Meditation," *IEEE Signal Processing Magazine* 25, no. 1 (January 1, 2008): 176.

Page 180: Deepak Chopra, *Reinventing the Body, Resurrecting the Soul: How to Create a New You* (New York: Random House, 2009).

Page 180: Dacher Keltner, *Born to be Good: The Science of a Meaningful Life* (New York: W.W. Norton & Co., 2009).

Page 181: Daniel Ladinsky, *Love Poems from God: Twelve Sacred Voices from the East and West* (New York: Penguin Books, 2002). Used by permission.

Page 186: Fran Peavey, Mrya Levy, and Charles Varon, *Heart Politics* (Philadelphia: New Society, 1986): 176.

Page 189: Coleman Barks, trans., *The Essential Rumi* (New York: HarperCollins, 1995). Used by permission.

Chapter 16

Page 191: Randy Pausch, "Last Lecture," Carnegie Mellon University, September 18, 2007, http://www.cmu.edu/randyslecture/.

Page 195: Katherine Woodward Thomas, *Calling in "The One": 7 Weeks to Attract the Love of Your Life* (New York: Three Rivers Press/Random House, 2004).

Chapter 17

Page 206: Desmond Tutu, Review of *Urgent Message from Mother: Gather the Women, Save the World,* by Jean Shinoda Bolen (San Francisco: Red Wheel/Weiser, 2009).

Page 206: Israel Shenker, "E. B. White: Notes and Comment by Author," *New York Times,* July 11, 1969.

Page 206: Martin E.P. Seligman, *Authentic Happiness: Using the New Positive Psychology to Realize Your Potential For Lasting Fulfillment* (New York: Atria/Simon & Schuster, 2002).

Page 207: Gabrielle Leblanc, "5 Things Happy People Do," *O, The Oprah Magazine*, March 2008: 233-235.

Page 207: Arianna Huffington, *On Becoming Fearless...In Love, Work, and Life* (New York: Little, Brown, 2006).

Page 208: Joan Duncan Oliver, "Kindness: The Ripple Effect," *O, The Oprah Magazine*, December 2002.

REFERENCES

Adamson, Edward. *Art As Healing.* London: Coventure, 1991.

Beck, Martha. "Martha Beck's Anti-Complain Campaign." *O, The Oprah Magazine,* October 2007.

Brockman, Max, ed. *What's Next? Dispatches on the Future of Science: Original Essays from a New Generation of Scientists.* New York: Vintage/Random House, 2009.

Buhner, Stephen. *Sacred Plant Medicine: The Wisdom in Native American Herbalism.* Rochester, VT: Inner Traditions, 2006.

Byers, Mary M. *How to Say No…and Live to Tell About It: A Woman's Guide to Guilt-Free Decisions.* Eugene, OR: Harvest House, 2006.

Cameron, Julia. *The Artist's Way: A Spiritual Path to Higher Creativity.* New York: Penguin Putnam, 1992.

Campbell, Susan. *Getting Real: Ten Truth Skills You Need to Live an Authentic Life.* Tiburon, CA: HJ Kramer, 2001.

Casey, Caroline. *Making the Gods Work for You: The Astrological Language of the Psyche.* New York: Three Rivers Press/Random House, 1998.

Chopra, Deepak. *Reinventing the Body, Resurrecting the Soul: How to Create a New You.* New York: Random House, 2009.

Chopra, Deepak. Interviewed on *The Ellen DeGeneres Show*, October 27, 2009.

Davidson, Richard, and Antoine Lutz. "Buddha's Brain: Neuroplasticity and Meditation." *IEEE Signal Processing Magazine* 25, no. 1 (January 1, 2008).

De Mille, Agnes. *Martha: The Life and Work of Martha Graham.* New York: Random House, 1991.

Ensler, Eve. *I Am an Emotional Creature: The Secret Life of Girls Around the World.* New York: Random House, 2010.

Fonda, Jane. *My Life So Far.* New York: Random House, 2005.

Gerzema, John. *The Athena Doctrine: How Women (and the Men Who Think Like Them) Will Rule the Future.* San Francisco: Jossey-Bass, 2013.

Gilbert, Elizabeth. *Eat, Pray, Love: One Woman's Search for Everything Across Italy, India and Indonesia.* New York: Penguin, 2007.

Hanh, Thich Nhat. *Fear: Essential Wisdom for Getting Through the Storm.* New York: HarperCollins, 2012.

Holden, Robert. *Happiness Now! Timeless Wisdom for Feeling Good FAST.* Carlsbad, CA: Hay House, 2007.

Huffington, Arianna. *On Becoming Fearless...In Love, Work, and Life.* New York: Little, Brown, 2006.

Keltner, Dacher. *Born to be Good: The Science of a Meaningful Life.* New York: W.W. Norton & Co., 2009.

Killingsworth, Matthew A., and Daniel T. Gilbert. "A Wandering Mind Is an Unhappy Mind." *Science* 330, no. 932 (November 12, 2010), DOI: 10.1126/science.1192439.

Leblanc, Gabrielle. "5 Things Happy People Do." *O, The Oprah Magazine,* March 2008.

Lipton, Bruce. *Spontaneous Evolution: Our Positive Future (And a Way to Get There from Here).* Carlsbad, CA: Hay House, 2009.

Morrisey, Mary Manin. *Building Your Field of Dreams.* New York: Bantam, 1997.

Murray, W.H. *The Scottish Himalayan Expedition.* London: J.M. Dent, 1951.

Oliver, Joan Duncan. "Kindness: The Ripple Effect." *O, The Oprah Magazine,* December 2002.

Openshaw, Jennifer. *The Millionaire Zone: Seven Winning Steps to a Seven-Figure Fortune.* New York: Hyperion, 2007.

Orloff, Judith. *Emotional Freedom: Liberate Yourself from Negative Emotions and Transform Your Life.* New York: Harmony/Random House, 2009.

Palmer, Wendy. *The Intuitive Body: Discovering the Wisdom of Conscious Embodiment and Aikido.* Berkeley, CA: Blue Snake Books/North Atlantic, 2008.

Pausch, Randy. "Last Lecture." Carnegie Mellon University, September 18, 2007. http://www.cmu.edu/randyslecture/.

Peavey, Fran, Mrya Levy, and Charles Varon. *Heart Politics.* Philadelphia: New Society, 1986.

Pink, Daniel. *A Whole New Mind: Why Right-Brainers Will Rule the Future.* London: Penguin, 2006.

Rich, Katherine Russell. "In a Single Stroke: The Metamorphosis of Jill Bolte Taylor." *O, The Oprah Magazine,* October 2002.

Salzberg, Sharon. *Faith: Trusting Your Own Deepest Experience.* New York: Riverhead, 2002.

Seligman, Martin E.P. *Authentic Happiness: Using the New Positive Psychology to Realize Your Potential For Lasting Fulfillment.* New York: Atria/Simon & Schuster, 2002.

Senge, Peter, C. Otto Scharmer, Joseph Jaworski, and Betty Sue Flowers. *Presence: Human Purpose and the Field of the Future.* New York: Doubleday, 2004.

Shenker, Israel. "E. B. White: Notes and Comment by Author." *New York Times,* July 11, 1969.

Shimoff, Marci. *Happy for No Reason: 7 Steps to Being Happy from the Inside Out.* New York: Free Press, 2009.

Stovall, Jim. *The Ultimate Gift.* Colorado Springs, CO: David C. Cook, 2001.

Thomas, Katherine Woodward. *Calling in "The One": 7 Weeks to Attract the Love of Your Life.* New York: Three Rivers Press/Random House, 2004.

Time. "Women's Liberation Revisited." March 20, 1972.

Tippett, Krista. "The Soul Checkup." *O, The Oprah Magazine,* May 2007.

Tutu, Desmond. Review of *Urgent Message from Mother: Gather the Women, Save the World,* by Jean Shinoda Bolen. San Francisco: Red Wheel/Weiser, 2009.

Williamson, Marianne. *A Return to Love: Reflections on the Principles of a Course in Miracles.* New York: HarperCollins, 1992.

Winfrey, Oprah. "Caroline Myss' Advice for Getting to the Heart of Who You Are." *O, The Oprah Magazine,* January 2013.

Winter, Jessica. "What Really Makes People Happy." *O, The Oprah Magazine,* May 2009.

INDEX

ABOUT THE AUTHOR

Wendy Wallbridge is a strategic and intuitive advisor to Fortune 100 leaders and teams across industries seeking breakthrough results, as well as a popular TEDx speaker. Recognized for her groundbreaking coaching techniques, she has been interviewed in print media including *Fortune* magazine, the *San Francisco Chronicle,* and the *New York Times.*

She is the producer of the TEDxSandHillRdWomen conference and the Women's Evolutionary Leadership Forum (WEL), whose sold-out events are attended by an audience of influential Silicon Valley women.

In 1993 Wendy founded On Your Mark Corporate Coaching & Consulting, Inc. when she saw the need for individuals to do work that was both meaningful to them and met the changing needs of the marketplace. On Your Mark's clients have included Intel, Hewlett-Packard, Apple, ABC-Disney, Wells Fargo, Oracle, Texas Instruments, Symantec, Genentech, Dolby, and McAfee, among others.

Wendy delivers keynotes, addresses, and seminars on self-empowerment and peak performance to corporations, women's associations, and professional and nonprofit organizations. She has taught her Spiral Up! principles for the past decade to groups of entrepreneurs, middle managers, individual contributors, and executives.

Please visit www.SpiralUp.com for additional resources, tools, and your complimentary leadership assessment to help you grow your impact as a leader.